AN INTRODUCTION TO
WEB SITE DESIGN

Mairi Mackinnon

Designed by Isaac Quaye

Managing designer: Russell Punter
Cover design by Zoë Wray

Illustrated by Christyan Fox and Isaac Quaye

Technical consultant: Sally Hughes
Managing editor: Jane Chisholm
With thanks to Susanna Davidson

TED SMART

Contents

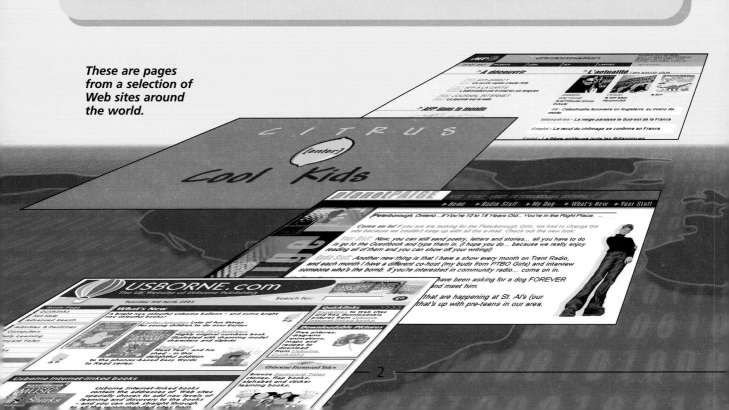

These are pages
from a selection of
Web sites around
the world.

About this book

This book tells you how to create and publish a site on the World Wide Web.

The World Wide Web, sometimes just called the Web, is the part of the Internet used by organizations and individuals to publish all kinds of information. Millions of people around the world have access to the Web. Most of the information on it can be seen by anybody, and most of it is free.

What is a Web site?

Information on the Web is shown in pages, like those below, and pages are grouped together as Web sites. Each site has its own unique address, usually beginning www. or http://www. This address is also known as a URL (Uniform Resource Locator), and tells your computer precisely where to find a particular site on the Web.

There are Web sites for all kinds of purposes. You can use the Web for research or homework help. Many bands, sports teams, movies or TV shows have Web sites for their fans. You can buy almost anything, from CDs to houses, on the Web. There are also sites to help you use the Web more efficiently, from finding the sites you want to getting hold of useful software.

Why build your own Web site?

A Web site is a great way of communicating with people. You might like to build a site for your family and friends, with news and photos. You might share a passion for a subject, such as pets or music or a place you know well. If you have a business, you may want to advertise your products or services.

You will see amazing sites on the Web with fantastic pictures, animations, sound clips and games. People can spend vast amounts of time and money on making their site look good. But you don't need to be a Web expert to produce a good basic site. This book shows you that it's easy to build a well-designed site of your own.

Does design matter?

There are billions of sites on the Web, and more are being added every day. There are no "design police" on the Web, in fact anyone can publish anything as long as it is legal. However, if you want people to enjoy visiting your site, you should try to make it as attractive and easy to use as you can. This book is full of tips to help you to do that, and examples of sites which are a pleasure to visit.

Usborne Quicklinks

This book contains references to around 100 Web sites, both as examples of good design and as places where you can find help or useful resources for designing your own site.

Web sites are being created, updated, moved and closed down all the time. In order to give you the most up-to-date links possible, we have placed links to all the sites on the Usborne Quicklinks Web site at **www.usborne-quicklinks.com**

For more about the Usborne Quicklinks site, and about using the Internet in general, see inside the front cover of this book.

What can a Web site do?

Web sites are created for different reasons – to share news and information, to sell products, to tell people about museums or charities, bands or sports teams. Here we have selected sites which were created for many different purposes, but they are all well-designed, attractive and easy to use. One of the best-looking was created by an 11-year-old boy to share his passion for drawing and painting.

If you want to look at these sites, you will find direct links to all of them at **www.usborne-quicklinks.com**

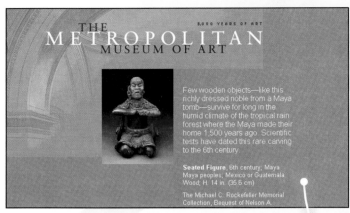

Web sites created by museums and art galleries are often beautifully designed. This is the Web site of the Metropolitan Museum of Art in New York.

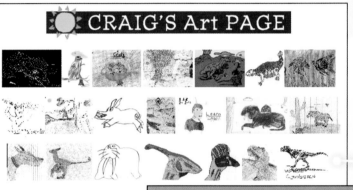

11-year-old Craig Williams created his own art gallery online.

Web sites for music fans often have "extras" such as sound and video clips. The band Teenage Fanclub has a Web site with details of tours and new releases.

Web sites for sports fans can give team news, player profiles and details of past and future games. Barcelona Football Club has a Web site in Spanish, Catalan or English.

Web sites offering information need to be clear and easy to use. You can find healthcare advice and a guide to the UK's National Health Service on the NHS Direct Web site.

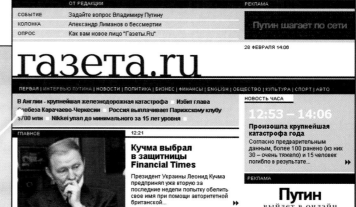

News sites can offer lots of information and publish news almost as soon as it happens. Gazeta is a Russian-language newspaper on the Internet.

Charities use the Internet to tell people about their causes and ask for their help. This is the Web site of the French medical aid organization Médecins Sans Frontières.

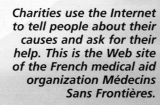

Web sites selling products or services should make them look bright and enticing. This Italian travel agency offers some inspiring destinations.

What do I need to get started?

To build a Web site of your own, you will need some basic hardware (computer equipment) and software (programs). You may be able to use your own computer, or you may have access to a computer at work, at school, in a library or an Internet café.

Your computer

You can use either a PC or a Macintosh computer to create a Web site. You don't need a brand-new or very powerful computer to build a basic Web site, but do make sure you can connect to the Internet easily.

Most Web site design software is designed for Microsoft® Windows® 95 or later versions of Windows, or Macintosh OS8.5 or later versions, so make sure you have one of these as your computer's operating system.

Your modem

Your modem is the device which connects your computer to the Internet via the telephone network. Your computer may have a built-in modem or you may use an external one, like the one above. In either case, your computer needs to be close to a telephone socket so that you can plug in your modem.

An external modem

It's a good idea to look at quite a few Web sites to give you ideas before you start. Make sure you don't have to spend too long downloading them (transferring them from the Internet to your computer for viewing). Downloading speed depends mainly on your modem, so it helps to have a fast modem, preferably 56K. There are other, faster ways of connecting to the Internet, but these tend to be expensive for home use.

Your Internet connection

To connect to the Internet, you need to have an account with an ISP (Internet Service Provider). Many ISPs offer you free Web space, which you can use for your Web site. If you are signing up with an ISP, ask whether they offer Web space.

Your computer should have a program called a browser. If not, your ISP will probably provide you with one. A browser is the program which allows you to find Web sites on the Internet and view them on your computer. It is also useful for checking your own Web site as you are designing it, so that you can see how it will finally look.

The most widely-used browsers are Netscape® Navigator (included with the Netscape® Communicator and Netscape® 6 series packages) and Microsoft® Internet Explorer.

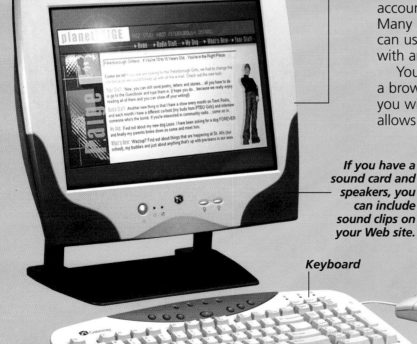

You can use an ordinary home PC to build your Web site.

Monitor

This PC has a built-in 56K modem. You can also use an external modem which you connect to your PC.

If you have a sound card and speakers, you can include sound clips on your Web site.

Keyboard

Mouse

Web design software

You can build a Web site in various ways. All Web sites are built up with a programming language called HTML (HyperText Mark-up Language). You can see what this looks like by using your browser to visit a Web site, then clicking on *View* and then *Source* (or *Page Source*) in your browser's toolbar. If you have never seen HTML before, it looks like gibberish, but in fact you can learn it fairly easily. You can find out more about HTML on pages 52-53.

There are much easier ways of creating a Web site, however. If you have Microsoft® Word on your computer, you can use Word to create a fairly basic Web page, in much the same way that you create a document for printing out. However, if you want to create a more sophisticated-looking page, you will want to use a Web editor.

Below you can see the Usborne Web site as it appears on screen, and the HTML code for the beginning of the home page.

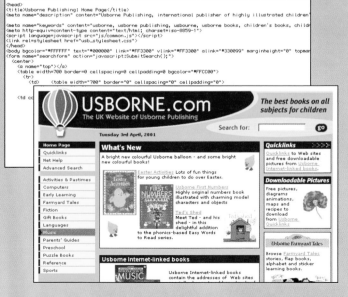

What is a Web editor?

A Web editor is a program which produces HTML but shows you on screen what the Web page will look like. This is known as WYSIWYG (What You See Is What You Get).

There are a number of popular Web editors to choose from. Microsoft® FrontPage®, the Web editor used in this book, is available in some countries as an inexpensive or free trial version for 30-45 days. After that, you can pay for the full version if you want to keep it. Netscape® Composer is a Web editor included free of charge with Netscape® Communicator and Netscape® 6 series.

When you have tried designing a Web page with a basic Web editor, you might like to look at one with more features. For example, Macromedia® Dreamweaver® is a Web editor which is popular with Web design professionals – you can find out more about it on page 54. It, too, is available as a free trial version.

You can obtain some of these editors via the Internet – there are links to some useful Web sites on the Usborne Quicklinks Web site at **www.usborne-quicklinks.com**

Dreamweaver is a Web editor often used by professional designers.

Planning your Web site

A Web editor makes it easy to start creating a Web site right away. Even so, it's worth spending a little time planning your site first, and collecting the material you want to use – text, pictures and so on.

Surfing for inspiration

The best place to get ideas for your Web site is on the Web itself. Look at a variety of Web sites, and decide which design ideas you like and which you think don't work so well. You may not have the same resources as the designers who created the sites, but you can still judge whether a site uses colours nicely or looks cluttered and complicated.

If you are not sure where to start looking, try some of the sites featured in this book. All these sites have been chosen as examples of effective Web design.

When you find a site you like, make sure that you can come back to it at a later date by bookmarking it (in Netscape) or adding it to your Favorites (Internet Explorer).

Collecting material

You can include all sorts of things on your Web site. The most common to start with are text and pictures, but you may want to add sound clips, video or animations as well. You can also have links to other sites you particularly like. Don't worry if you don't have all your material ready right away. You can always add more pages to your site later.

It's a good idea to have a special folder on your computer for all the things you plan to put on your site. This makes it easy to find and place pictures or other elements when you are designing your site. When you come to upload your site (publish it on the Internet), you will need to send a lot of this material to the ISP or other organization which is hosting it, too.

The best place to create this folder is in the My Documents folder, which you can see on your computer's desktop on the left-hand side of the screen. When you are saving files for your Web site, make sure each file has a different name. It's best to make file names no more than eight characters long.

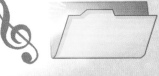

Copyright

While you are surfing other people's sites, you may see some great pictures and animations. Don't be tempted to copy these for use on your own site, however. Pictures and information generally belong to the person who created them, or to an organization representing that person. This is called "intellectual property" or "copyright".

Some pictures are available for anyone to use. You can find out more about "copyright-free" pictures on page 14. If you want to use any other pictures or text you have found, you must get permission from the person or company that owns the copyright. If you don't do this, you may be breaking the law.

Thumbnail sketches help you to plan your site.

Mapping out your site

When you have decided what you want to include on your Web site, you may find that you have enough material for several pages or more. Think about how you will organize the site. You will need to create a "home page" – an introductory page that tells visitors what information your site contains, and that has links to other pages on the site.

Divide your material between pages. Don't be tempted to put too much on one page. It's much more effective to share the content between several shorter pages instead.

It's a good idea to group different kinds of information. For example, lots of Web sites include a picture gallery, with a collection of pictures or photos on one page. (You can find out more about picture galleries on page 25.) If you are including links to other sites, you can keep them all together on a "links" page.

This is a fairly typical home page.

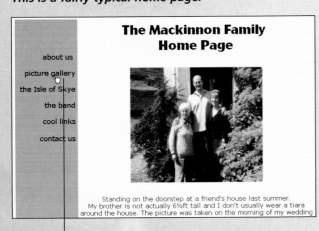

The Mackinnon Family Home Page

about us
picture gallery
the Isle of Skye
the band
cool links
contact us

Standing on the doorstep at a friend's house last summer. My brother is not actually 6½ft tall and I don't usually wear a tiara around the house. The picture was taken on the morning of my wedding

These are links to other pages on the site.

Designing page layout

Try sketching the pages of your site on paper. Quick sketches called "thumbnails", like the ones shown above, can help you decide where to put text and pictures. Think about a general theme or mood for your site, and how you might create this – by using similar colours, for example, or similar designs on different pages.

There are a few things to remember when you are planning page layout. People download Web sites to different computers, and different screen sizes may not show your whole page width. Put important information, such as the page title, where it can easily be seen (towards the top of the page, on the left or in the centre). Don't put links on the right of the page where they may be overlooked. If you are using text, don't make the text area too wide.

Above all, avoid putting too many pictures, animations or other "extras" on your home page. This will make the page take a long time to download, which is frustrating for visitors to your site.

⚠ Be safe

Millions of Internet users will be able to see the information on your Web site. If you are creating a personal site, don't include anything private, such as your home address or telephone number.

Your first Web page

Once you are ready to start creating Web pages, find and open your Web editor. The Web editor used in this book is Microsoft® FrontPage®.

If you have Microsoft® Office installed on your computer, it may already include a copy of FrontPage. Click on the Start button at the bottom left-hand corner of your screen, then on Programs, and look for Microsoft FrontPage in the list that comes up. Click on it to open the program.

If you don't have FrontPage already installed, you may be able to order a trial copy from Microsoft. Go to **www.usborne-quicklinks.com** to find out more.

Introducing FrontPage

If you are familiar with Microsoft® Word, you will find that FrontPage looks similar and many tools and commands are the same. As in Word, if you let your cursor rest over a button or symbol, a label will appear telling you what it is.

When you open FrontPage, you will see an empty window like the one shown below.*

The opening window looks like this.

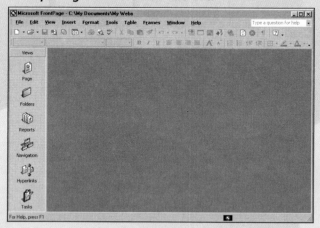

Click on *File* in the top left-hand corner of the screen, then on *New* and then *Page or Web...* in the drop-down menus that appear. Select Empty Web and then One Page Web from the options given, and click *OK*. Then click on the blank paper icon at the top left-hand corner of the screen.

A basic home page

Try creating a basic home page using FrontPage. Your page will need a title, and you may also like to include a little information about yourself. You can add a picture or other decoration later, if you like.

Double-click on the icon entitled index.htm in the Folder List on the left of the FrontPage window. In the page area on the right, type your page title and a short introductory piece, as on the page below.

The folder list shows you all the files and folders that make up your Web site. You can close and open it by clicking this button.

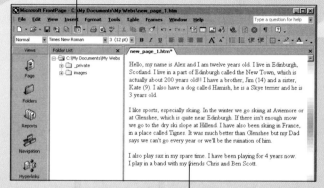

This is how your page might look.

Now you can try formatting the text a little. Select a piece of text by highlighting it with your mouse. You can then make it bold, centre it or change the size.

Click here to change the size of your highlighted text, and select a text size.

Click here for bold.

Click here to centre your highlighted text.

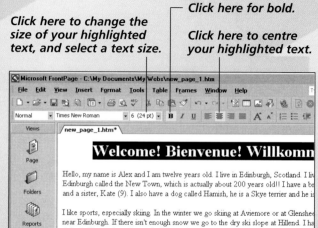

*FrontPage 2000 and earlier versions open directly on to a blank Web page.

Saving your Web page

As with any work you do on your computer, you should save your Web page often. FrontPage automatically saves your page in a special folder so that you can find it and open it again easily another time.

Saving your page

To save your page, click on *File* in the Menu bar at the top of the screen, and click on *Save* in the drop-down menu that appears.

Click here.

The first time you do this, a Save As window will appear, like the one below. Your page will be saved as index.htm, which indicates that it is your site's home page. The page title (which will appear at the top of the browser window when the page is published) is given as Home Page, but you can change it if you like by clicking on *Change...* Then click on *Save*.

When you click on *Save* again, your page will automatically be saved with the same settings.

The Save As window

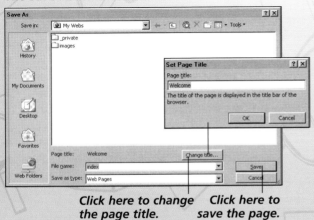

Click here to change the page title.   **Click here to save the page.**

Closing and reopening your page

FrontPage saves your page in a folder called My Webs, which is in the My Documents folder. You can now close down FrontPage, but you will still be able to go back to your page and open it again.

When you reopen FrontPage, click on *File* and then on *Open...* in the drop-down menu that appears. Alternatively, click on the opening folder icon in the toolbar below the menu bar.

Click here.

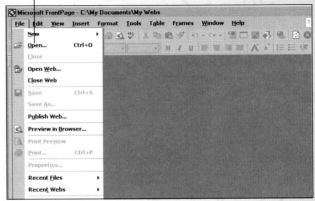

FrontPage will show you all the files in My Webs, including your saved page. Click on *Open...* or double-click on the filename to open the page.

Here is your saved page.

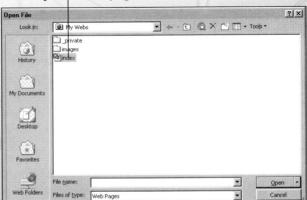

Changing text

You can vary the appearance of text on a Web page to make it easier to read. By dividing up blocks of text, and choosing the right typeface, you can make your page look better and more attractive altogether.

Breaking up blocks of text

Text is generally harder to read on screen than it is on the page of a book, so think how to make it easier for visitors to your site. Large blocks of text are difficult and tiring to read, so use lots of short paragraphs rather than a few long ones.

When you finish a paragraph, press the Return key. Microsoft® FrontPage® will automatically insert a line space before the next paragraph. You can see this in the first page below.

(If for any reason you *don't* want a line space, hold down the Shift key and then press the Return key.)

This page is much easier to read...

> **index.htm***
>
> Hello, my name is Alex and I am twelve years old. I live in Edinburgh, Scotland. I live in a part of Edinburgh called the New Town, which is actually about 200 years old!! I have a brother, Jim (14) and a sister, Kate (9). I also have a dog called Hamish, he is a Skye terrier and he is 3 years old.
>
> I like sports, especially skiing. In the winter we go skiing at Aviemore or at Glenshee, which is quite near Edinburgh. If there isn't enough snow we go to the dry ski slope at Hillend. I have also been skiing in France, in a place called Tignes. It was much better than Glenshee but my Dad says we can't go every year or we'll be the ruination of him.
>
> I also play sax in my spare time. I have been playing for 4 years now. I play in a band with my friends Chris and Ben. Chris plays keyboards, she is really good. She goes to a school that has a special music and dance unit. Ben plays drums, he is quite good but he doesn't keep time very well, which is a big problem if you are a drummer. We try to play
>
> Normal HTML Preview

> lay in
>
> good. She goes to a school that has a special music and dance unit. Ben plays drums, he is quite good but he doesn't keep time very well, which is a big problem if you are a drummer. We try to play every weekend but it doesn't always work out, especially if Ben is playing rugby, he is in the junior team at his school so he quite often has a game. Another friend, Sam, used to play bass but he went to live in England so we are looking for a bass player at the moment. Last summer we all went on music camp in Aberdeen. We had a brilliant time and met some other really good bands. I like listening to famous sax players like Stan Getz. I wish I could play like that, though my teacher says it's OK if you're Stan Getz but mere mortals like you and I have to play by the book and don't you forget it young Alex. My teacher is excellent, he is always making me laugh, he always pretends to be grumpy but he isn't really.
>
> Normal HTML Preview

...than this one.

Different sizes and styles

On page 10, you saw how to increase type size, and make type bold. These are good ways of making a piece of text stand out, for example as a page title or a heading.

There are seven sizes of type you can use on a Web page. They are shown below.

These are the various type sizes you can use for text.

This is size one

This is size two

This is size three

This is size four

This is size five

This is size six

and size seven

You can also use bold, italic and underlined type. However, bear in mind that italic type can be hard to read on screen, and underlining is generally used for hyperlinks, so to save confusion, avoid using it for other purposes.

Using different type sizes, and maybe bold type for titles and headings, can make a Web page look more interesting and readable.

> **index.htm***
>
> ### Welcome! Bienvenue! Willkommen!
>
> **About me**
> Hello, my name is Alex and I am twelve years old. I live in Edinburgh, Scotland. I live in a part of Edinburgh called the New Town, which is actually about 200 years old!! I have a brother, Jim (14) and a sister, Kate (9). I also have a dog called Hamish, he is a Skye terrier and he is 3 years old.
>
> **My music**
> I also play sax in my spare time. I have been playing for 4 years now. I play in a band with my friends Chris and Ben. Chris plays keyboards, she is really good. She goes to a school that has a special music and dance unit. Ben plays drums, he is quite good but he doesn't keep time very well, which is a big problem if you are a drummer. We try to play
>
> Normal HTML Preview

The section headings on the page above are a size bigger than the main text, and are in bold type.

Changing the font

You can make a piece of text more readable by changing the typeface, or font. You may have quite a few fonts installed on your own computer, but other computers will only display text using the fonts they have, so it's best not to use anything too individual and unusual.

There are three main kinds of fonts:

Display fonts These are very decorative, and are good for making headings or key words stand out on paper, but not all computers have the same ones, so they are not ideal for Web pages. Some examples of display fonts are:

COPPERPLATE GOTHIC

MATISSE   **Adelaide**

Serif fonts These are probably the most often-used fonts you will find in books and newspapers. "Serifs" are the little points on the ends of the letters. Some examples of serif fonts are:

Garamond

Palatino   Times

Sans serif fonts These fonts, without serifs, have a more modern feel. They are also generally easier to read on a computer screen. Some examples of sans serif fonts are:

Arial

Helvetica   Verdana

Verdana is a font developed especially for using in Web pages as it is especially easy to read on screen. If you have it on your computer, it might be a good one to use on your page.

To change the font in FrontPage, highlight a section of text and then click in the middle box in the formatting toolbar immediately above the page. Choose a font from the drop-down menu which appears.

Click here to select a font.

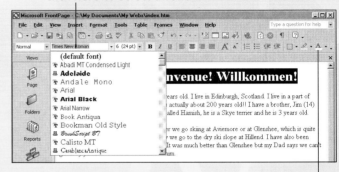

Click here to change the font colour.

Changing the font colour

You can also make text look more interesting by changing the colour. You do this by highlighting the text and clicking on the little black arrow beside the capital A in the formatting toolbar. This gives you a drop-down menu with a range of sixteen standard colours. You can click on *More Colors...* at the bottom of the menu for more choices.

You can have fun with different colours, but don't get carried away – too many colours will only be distracting. You can find some advice on combining colours on page 56.

This page, with dark blue text on a light blue background, using a sans serif font, is easy to read. The page below it is a mess!

Abair ach beagan agus abair gu math e • An rud a nithear gu math, chithear a bhuil • An uair a chluinneas tu sgeul gun dreach na creid i • Am fear a bhios fad aig an aiseig, gheibh e thairis uaireigin • A bheairt sin a bhios cearr, 'se foighidinn is fhear a dheanamh ris • An rud nach gabh leasachadh, 's feudar cur suas leis • Bu mhath an sgàthan sùil caraid • Bheir an eigin air rudeigin a dheanamh • Bheirear comhairle Beiridh caora dhubh uan gea dh an ùbhal is fhear r a phoit

Putting pictures on your Web page

You can personalize your page and make it look more interesting by adding pictures. You can either use copyright-free pictures from the Internet, or prepare pictures of your own for placing on a Web page. These two pages tell you how to find and use ready-prepared pictures.

Clip art

Clip art is the name for pictures that you can use in personal documents. It is generally free of charge, and you don't have to ask permission from the artist or owner unless you are using the pictures for a commercial site. You should always credit the artist or owner, though (by giving their name underneath the picture). Some clip art sites ask you to include a link back to their site. You can find out how to do this on page 21.

Where to find clip art

Microsoft® FrontPage® includes a selection of basic clip art pictures, but you will find many, many more on the Internet. You might start by looking on one of the sites listed below, or you could use a search engine (type in the search terms **free web clip art**).

Clip art sites

You'll find links to some useful clip art sites on the Usborne Quicklinks site, at **www.usborne-quicklinks.com**

For example, there are huge collections of images on the Web sites of **Clipart.com**, **Barry's Clipart Server** and **Clip Art Connection**. You'll also find some fun images at the **Clip Art Warehouse** Web site.

If you want to use photos on your site, there's a superb collection at **Freefoto.com**. Freefoto pictures are free to use on personal Web sites, but check the instructions for crediting them on the Usborne Quicklinks Web site.

Selecting and saving pictures

When you have found a picture that you like, save it from the Internet to your own computer by clicking on it with the right-hand button of your mouse. (If you are using a Macintosh computer, click and hold down your mouse button.) A menu will appear like the one below.

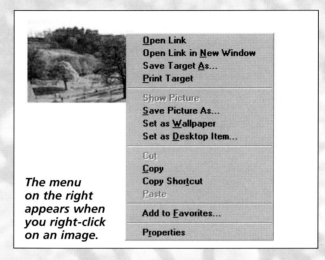

The menu on the right appears when you right-click on an image.

Click on *Save Picture As...* and a Save Picture window will appear, like the one below. Your browser will automatically give the picture a file name, and save it into the My Pictures folder in My Documents. You can change the file name if you want. Then click on *Save*.

The Save Picture window

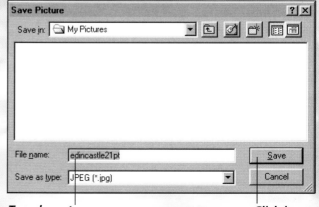

Type here to change the file name.

Click here to save the picture.

Placing pictures on your page

Once you have the pictures you want to use, it is easy to place them on your Web page. Make sure that they are not too big – the files should be under 40 kilobytes (KB) in size. If you are not sure how big a picture file is, you can check by opening up the My Pictures folder in My Documents and clicking on the file. In the left-hand part of the window you will see details of the file, including its size, as below.

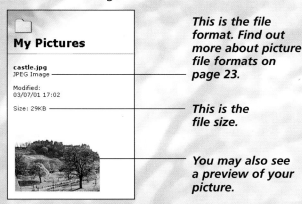

This is the file format. Find out more about picture file formats on page 23.

This is the file size.

You may also see a preview of your picture.

Now open up your Web page in FrontPage. Choose where on the page you would like your picture to appear, place the cursor at the end of the line before and press the return key (to give the picture enough space between lines of text). Check that the cursor is in the right position on the page – you can place a picture on the left, the middle or the right of a page by clicking on the text alignment buttons in the formatting toolbar.

Click on these buttons to position the picture.

The cursor shows you the picture will be centred.

Now select the picture you want to use. Click on *Insert* in the menu bar and then on *Picture* and then *From File...* in the drop-down menu that appears. A window will appear like the one below.

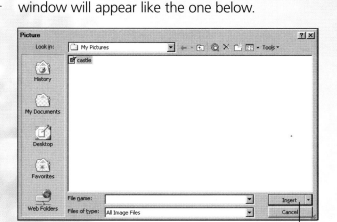

Click here to place your picture on the page.

Click on My Documents, open My Pictures and select your picture. Click on *Insert*, and FrontPage will place it on your Web page.

If you want to make the picture larger or smaller, click on it. You will see eight black dots around its edges. Click and drag one of the dots on the corners until the picture is the right size.

Finally, remember to insert a credit below the picture. (You can make the type a size or two smaller than your main text.)

This is how your page might look once you have inserted the picture and credit.

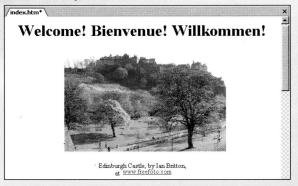

When you come to save your page, you will see that FrontPage also saves the picture separately into My Webs, as an "embedded file".

Backgrounds and colour

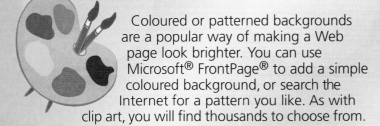

Coloured or patterned backgrounds are a popular way of making a Web page look brighter. You can use Microsoft® FrontPage® to add a simple coloured background, or search the Internet for a pattern you like. As with clip art, you will find thousands to choose from.

Changing the background colour

The default background (the standard one used until you make any changes) in FrontPage is white, and the text is black. Page 13 described one way of changing the text colour. You can also change default text and background colours by using the *Format Background* commands.

Open up your Web page in FrontPage. Click on *Format* in the menu bar, and a drop-down menu will appear. Click on *Background...* in this menu, and a Page Properties window will open like the one below.

Click here to change the background colour.

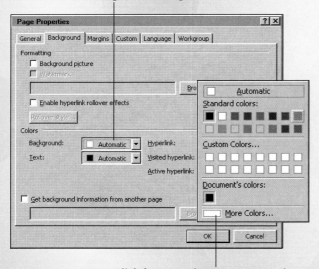

Click here to choose a new colour.

In the Colors section of the window, click on the box beside *Background* to change the background colour. As with the text, you will be offered a choice of sixteen standard colours, but you may prefer to mix your own. To do this, click on *More Colors...* in the box at the bottom of the colour menu.

Mixing a new colour

When you select *More Colors...*, you will see a window like the one below, with a choice of 133 more colours. Click on any of the hexagons to select that colour, and then click *OK*.

You can choose any of these colours.

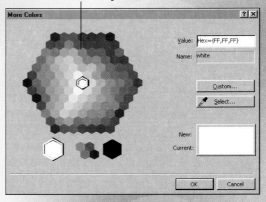

For a bigger range of colours still, click on *Custom...* to define your colour. A window will appear like the one below.

Select a colour from the spectrum... **...and a shade from the bar on the right.**

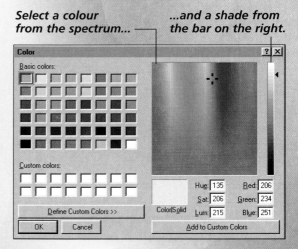

Click on the first box below *Custom Colors:* and then select a colour from the spectrum panel. You can make it darker or lighter by moving the black arrow beside the shade bar on the right. When you are happy with the colour, click on *Add to Custom Colors* and then on *OK*. You will return to the More Colors window; click on *OK*, and then *OK* again in the Page Properties window.

Changing the text colour

Your Web page might now look something like the first page below. You can also use the same method to change the default text colour, as on the second page.

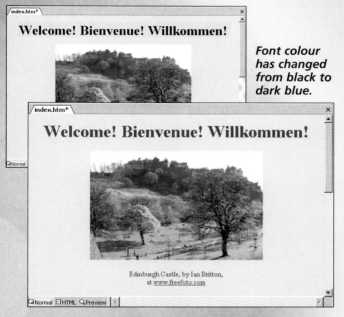

Font colour has changed from black to dark blue.

Patterned backgrounds

You can find backgrounds on the Internet in the same way that you can find clip art. Try the sites below, or use a search engine (use the search terms **web design background**). Remember to credit the background designer and include a link to their page if they ask you to.

Backgrounds are fun to use, but choose them very carefully. A fussy, heavily-patterned background makes text difficult to read, and can actually make your page look *less* attractive.

Background sites

Go to **www.usborne-quicklinks.com** for links to collections of backgrounds, such as the huge range at **Barracuda Backgrounds**. There are patterns for all occassions at **The Background Boutique**, too.

Placing a background on your page

When you have found a background you like, save it into the My Pictures folder by right-clicking on it, as described for the clip art picture on page 14.

To place it on the page, go back to your page in FrontPage and click on *Format – Background...*, as you did on the page opposite for a plain-coloured background. In the Page Properties window which appears, click on the box next to *Background picture*, then click on the Browse button to locate the background you have saved.

Click here to select a background.

Click here to find the background image.

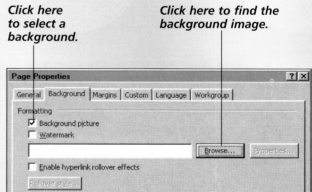

Find the file in My Pictures, as you did on page 15, and click OK and OK again. Your page will appear with its background, as below. When you save the page, FrontPage will also save the background image separately into My Webs.

This is the page with the background in place.

Personal home pages

You can find huge numbers of personal home pages through a directory such as Yahoo!® Try Yahooligans! for a selection of home pages created by children. You'll find plenty of design disasters, but also some really effective pages.

The examples on this page were created by families and individuals in different countries around the world. You can find links to them, and to directories of personal home pages, at **www.usborne-quicklinks.com**

The Web site of the Nieukerke family in Holland is a way for them to keep in touch with friends and family around the world.

The Bertacci site has a (none too recent) portrait of its creator, and his home town, Oleggio, in Italy.

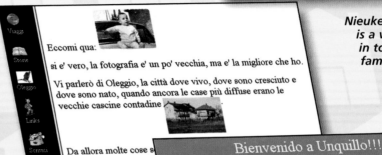

The stunning "Vrai Millenaire" site was created by a group of students in Camuy, Puerto Rico, graduating from high school in in the "real Millennium" year, 2001.

Part of a site created by Gustavo Bazán and his wife and dedicated to their home town of Unquillo, Argentina

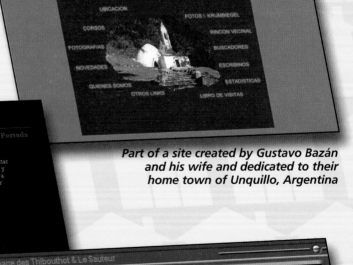

A picture gallery page created by the Thiboutot family, in Canada

The Reinhardt family's page design is simple and elegant.

Josep Fornell uses his home page to tell people about his rally driving team in Catalonia, Spain.

Amy Miller Gray's site: not afraid of the big issues

Benjamin Camara has created an impressive Web site in French (left) and English (above).

Adding pages and creating links

Once you know how to set up a Web page, you can easily create more pages and link them to the original.

Starting a new page

To create a new page in Microsoft® FrontPage®, all you have to do is click on the blank paper icon in the top left-hand corner of the screen. If you are working on an existing page, save it and close it first. Do this by clicking on *File* – *Save* and then *File* – *Close* in the menu bar. Then open a new page by clicking on the blank paper icon.

Click here to open a new page.

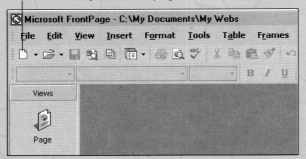

Save the page, as you did on page 11, and change its file name if you like. FrontPage will save the new page, as well as any new pictures, into My Webs.

You could create a page all about your home town.

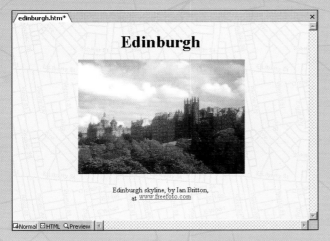

Creating a navigation structure

When you have more than one page for your site, you need to incorporate them in a structure which will keep all the pages together. You can do this by using the Navigation view in the Views bar to add on to your home page.

Click on Navigation at the left-hand side of the FrontPage window. You will see a window like the one below, with the Folder List on the left and an area on the right containing your home page. (The latest versions of FrontPage automatically place your new page in the same navigation structure as your home page, and you will see it in the area on the right as well.)

Click here to see your site's navigation structure.

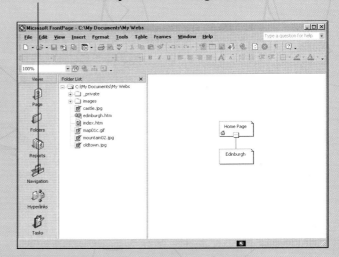

If you only see your home page in the area on the right, you will need to add your new page to the site's structure. Click on your new page in the Folders List, hold your mouse button down and drag it into the area on the right. You will see a grey line linking it to your home page. Make sure that your new page is below the home page, then release the mouse button.

You will now see both pages in the Navigation area, linked by a solid blue line. To go back and work on your page, click on Page in the Views bar.

You can create and add more pages to your site in the same way.

Linking to your new page

Once you have placed your new page in the navigation structure, you need to create a link to it from your home page.

Start by opening your home page. You can link either a word or a picture to your new page. Highlight the word you want to link, or select the picture, then click on the Hyperlink button in the Toolbar. An Insert Hyperlink window will appear.

Select the item you want to link, and click on this symbol to create a hyperlink.

This will be the link.

Click on your new page to link it.

In the list of files, click on the filename of your new page. The filename will appear in the *Address:* box. Click *OK*.

If you have linked a word to your new page, you will now see it in blue type and underlined. This shows visitors that it is a hyperlink.

Save your page. To see that the link is working, you can click on the Preview tab at the bottom left-hand corner of the FrontPage window. This shows you how your page will appear when published. When you click on the link, you will be taken directly to your new page.

Linking to another Web site

Links between pages of a Web site are called local links. Links from one Web site to another are called remote links, and you create them in much the same way.

For example, you might want to insert a hyperlink as part of a credit if you have used clip art or backgrounds from another Web site. First type in your credit (check the Web site to see if there is any specific wording you should use) and the URL of the site. Highlight the URL, and click on the Hyperlink button in the Toolbar. An Insert Hyperlink window will appear.

Type the site's URL into this box.

The hyperlink appears in blue and underlined.

Type the site's URL into the *Address* box – be sure to type it correctly – then click *OK*. The link will appear on your main page in blue and underlined. If you are online, you can check it using the Preview tab, as for a local link.

You can also make a picture into a remote link – you might do this if a site asks you to show its logo as part of a credit. Save the logo from the original site and place it as you would clip art (see page 15). Then click on it to select it, and create the hyperlink as above.

When you view the page using the Preview tab, you can tell that the logo is a hyperlink because your mouse cursor turns into a pointing hand when it is over the logo.

Preparing your own pictures

Once you know how to place pictures on your Web page, you can try using pictures of your own. To do this, you will need to prepare them as digital images that you can store on your computer. Digital images are pictures converted into number code that your computer reads in order to display the picture.

Image resolution

A picture on a computer is divided into tiny dots called pixels. Each pixel is one single colour, but they are so tiny that when you see the whole picture, the colours blend together smoothly. The digital image file tells your computer the exact colour and position of each pixel.

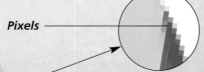

Pixels

This part of the picture has been enlarged so that you can see the pixels.

Digital images can be saved in different ways, and some picture file formats are more suitable for Web pages than others. The more pixels a picture is divided into, the more smoothly the colours blend. The number of pixels is known as resolution, and is measured in dots per inch (dpi).

A high-resolution picture looks very sharp and clear, but takes up a lot of memory space on a computer. A low-resolution picture takes up less space, but may look fuzzy. If you are printing a picture out on paper, you generally need to print at high resolution, but pictures on a Web page will look fine at a low resolution of 72 dpi.

On the right you can see the difference between a high-resolution and a low-resolution image.

Preparing digital images

There are several ways of creating digital images. If you create the image in a computer graphics program, such as Microsoft® Paint, it will automatically be saved in digital form. As long as you save it in the right file format (see opposite), you can then place it directly on a Web page.

If you have a digital camera, it will save the photos you take in digital form. You can download the photos from the camera to your computer, using the special software supplied with the camera. You can use the software to convert the picture into the right file format. You may also need to compress it by reducing the resolution.

A digital camera

You can also convert photographs or drawings you have into digital form by using a scanner. A scanner works a little like a photocopier, but produces a digital image file rather than an actual copy from your original. Top quality scanners for printing and publishing cost a lot of money, but

A scanner

you can buy inexpensive basic versions for home use. Many photocopying bureaux also have scanners that you can use for a small charge.

This is a high-resolution image. It was scanned in at 300 dpi.

This is a low-resolution image. It was scanned in at 72 dpi.

Picture file format

The more memory space a picture uses, the longer it will take to download on a Web page. To save downloading time, picture files are either simplified or compressed (made smaller).

Two of the commonest picture file formats for Web pages are GIF files and JPEG files. GIF files are good for simple pictures in basic colours, such as cartoons, as they keep files small by using a maximum of 256 colours. GIF files are also good for icons – small pictures which represent something else, such as a link to another part of your site.

These icons are GIF files. GIF files are suitable for simple images using a limited range of colours.

JPEG files are often used for photographs and pictures with a lot of detail, as they can include more colours than GIFs but can be compressed to take up very little space.

These are JPEG images. JPEG files are best for more complex images, such as photographs.

Saving files as GIFs

When you save a picture in a graphics program, you can choose to save it as a GIF. When you click on *File* and then *Save As...*, you will see a Save As window like the one below. In the box *Save as type,* select GIF (or Graphics Interchange Format) from the options you are given. Your image file will have a file name ending in .gif

The Save As window

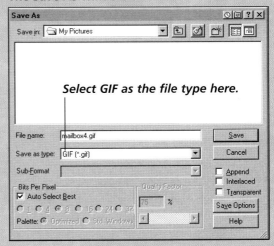

Select GIF as the file type here.

Saving files as JPEGs

You can save a picture as a JPEG in the same way, by selecting the file type JPEG (or JPEG File Interchange Format). Your file will have a name ending in .jpg

Some graphics programs allow you to alter the amount a JPEG file is compressed. This means that you can make the file smaller, but the image quality won't be quite as good. Try saving different versions of your picture, compressed by different amounts. When you place the picture on your Web page, use the Preview tab to see what it will look like. Use the smallest sized file that still looks good. In any case, try to keep picture files under 40KB in size.

Using your pictures

You can place your pictures on your Web page in the same way as you placed clip art on pages 14-15. These pages will also show you a few more ways you can use pictures to make your page more interesting.

Creating a hotspot

With Microsoft® FrontPage®, you can choose to make just one area of a picture into a hyperlink. For example, the page below is a welcome page for a band Web site. To reach the rest of the site, you have to click on the bird in the logo (which has been saved as a GIF file).

Click on the image and use one of these three buttons to create a hotspot.

Place your picture, then click on it to select it. Click on one of the Create Hotspot buttons in the Pictures toolbar at the bottom of the screen. If you are using the rectangular or circular hotspot buttons, click at one corner of the area you want to make into a hotspot, and drag the cursor until you have enclosed the area. If you are using the polygonal hotspot button, click on points all around the area you want to enclose.

When you have fully enclosed your hotspot area, a Create Hyperlink window will appear, as on page 21. Select the Web page you want to link to, and click *OK*.

Using icons

Icons are a great way of making a Web page look brighter without making it take a long time to download. This makes them especially useful on a home page, which should download quickly but still look attractive.

You can either use icons from a clip art gallery (see page 14 for the names of some clip art sites), or create your own. Try creating simple icons in a graphics program such as Microsoft® Paint, or scan in simple drawings and save them as GIF files. Keep them small – they should appear on your Web page at about 15mm^2.

The home page below uses home-produced icons as hyperlinks to other areas of the site. The hyperlinks are also given in words, in case the icon meanings aren't clear. You make the icons and their descriptions into hyperlinks in the same way as on page 21.

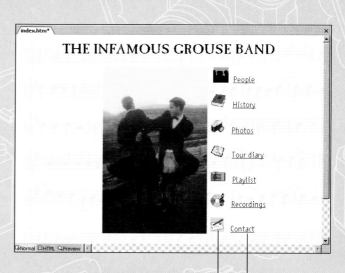

Both the icons and their descriptions act as hyperlinks to other pages on the site.

The page also includes a home-produced background (hand-written sheet music, scanned in and saved as a GIF file) and a single photo. You can find out how to place a photo with text beside it like this on the page opposite.

Wrapping text around a picture

When you tried placing a picture on page 15, you had the option of placing it on the left, in the middle or on the right of your Web page. If you place a picture in this way, you will find that you can't place more than one line of text alongside it. If you want to place a picture in text, as on the page below, you need to tell FrontPage to wrap the text around it.

This page has text wrapped around a picture.

Open your page of text, and place the picture at the beginning of the main text block. Click on the picture to select it, then click on *Format* in the Menu bar and then *Position...* from the drop-down menu which appears. You will see a window like the one below. Under *Wrapping style*, click on *Left*, and your picture will be positioned to the left of your text. You can then adjust the picture size by clicking and dragging the points at its corners, until you are happy with the look of your page.

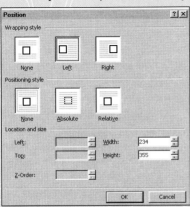

The text wrap Position window

Creating a picture gallery

You might like to show a collection of pictures together on a picture gallery page. Normally, if you put too many pictures together on a page, it makes the page very slow to download. You can avoid this, though, by showing the pictures in mini versions called thumbnails. If you click on a thumbnail, another page will open showing a full-sized version.

FrontPage makes it easy to create thumbnails. First, place all the pictures you want on your picture gallery page. Click on a picture to select it, and then click on the Auto Thumbnail button in the Pictures toolbar at the bottom of the screen. FrontPage will turn the picture into a thumbnail, with a blue outline which shows that it is a hyperlink (to the page with the full-sized version of the picture). You can resize the thumbnail as you would a normal picture, by clicking and dragging the corner points.

When you come to save the page, FrontPage will also save both versions of each image – the thumbnail and the full-size version.

Click here to turn an image into a thumbnail.

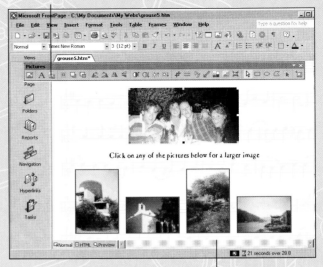

These four images are all thumbnails.

User-friendly Web pages

You can add elements to your site to make it more welcoming and easy to navigate. For example, you can create a special link to allow visitors to e-mail you, or add a counter to track visits. You can also help visitors to find your site, and find their way around when they get there.

Creating an e-mail link

Many Web sites include a link that people can click on to contact the site owner. Generally, this is via e-mail, although commercial Web sites may also include business addresses and phone numbers. Clicking on an e-mail link creates an e-mail pre-addressed to you, which your visitors can then complete and send.

In Microsoft® FrontPage®, you create an e-mail link in much the same way as you create any hyperlink (see pages 20-21). Highlight the text or select the icon you want to make into an e-mail link, then click on the Create Hyperlink button in the Toolbar. An Insert Hyperlink window will appear. Click on the small envelope symbol at the bottom of the window, and an E-mail Address window will appear over the Insert Hyperlink window. Type your e-mail address, then click *OK*.

Click here to create an e-mail link.

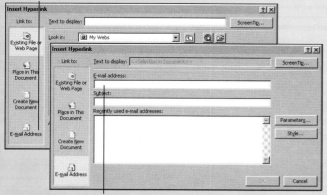

Type your e-mail address in this box.

To see the link working, click on the Preview tab at the bottom of the main FrontPage window, then click on your e-mail link. Like your visitors, you will see a blank e-mail pre-addressed to you.

> ⚠ **Nuisance e-mail**
>
> Remember, if you put an e-mail address on your Web site, anyone at all who sees your site can use it. There is a risk that people might send you rude or annoying messages.
>
> Before you give an e-mail address, see whether your e-mail account has a facility for filtering or blocking messages from nuisance senders. Never reply to a nuisance message, just delete it and block the sender.

Inserting a hit counter

A hit counter is a popular way of keeping track of visits to your site: it's fun to be able to see on the site itself how many visits your site has received. FrontPage includes several styles of hit counter you can choose from, and it's easy to place one on your home page. You will only be able to use one if your ISP supports FrontPage Extensions, though (find out more about FrontPage Extensions on page 31).

Place the cursor on your home page where you want the counter to appear. You could introduce it with the words "You are visitor number", or something similar. Then click on *Insert* in the Menu bar, and then on *Web*

component and then *Hit Counter* in the menus which appear. Choose the counter style you prefer, and click *Finish* then *OK*.

You can choose from these counter styles in FrontPage.

On your page, you will see the words **[Hit Counter]** but, even when you use the Preview tab, you will not actually see the counter yet. It will appear when you come to publish your page on the Internet.

Inserting keywords

When you publish your Web site, you can arrange for more people to see it by submitting it to a few search engines. Most search engines find sites by looking for keywords – words which describe what the site is all about. These don't appear as such on the site, but are hidden in the HTML code near the top of the page, where a search engine can find them easily.

You'll find more about submitting your site to search engines on page 47, but it's a good idea to insert keywords at this stage, before you publish your site. Search engines generally allow up to fifteen keywords. You can choose keywords for each page of your site, if you like (different pages will then show as results for different search terms), or just for your home page.

To insert keywords, first open your page. Click on *File* in the menu bar and then on *Properties* in the drop-down menu which appears. Click on the Custom tab in the Page Properties window which appears. In the *User variables* section, click on *Add...* You will see a window like the one below.

Type keywords **in this box**

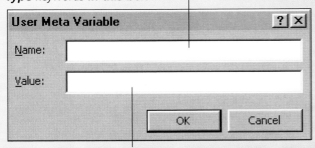

Type your keywords in here, separated by commas.

In the *Name* box, type **keywords**. In the *Value* box, type your keywords, separated by commas. Then click *OK*, and then *OK* again.

You will not see the keywords on your page in the Normal page view, but you can check that they are there by clicking on the HTML tab at the bottom left-hand corner of the FrontPage window. About five or six lines from the top, you will see `<meta name="keywords" content=` with the keywords you have chosen.

Setting bookmarks

You can set up a hyperlink within a single page of your Web site. On a long page, for example, it's useful for visitors to be able to go back to the top of the page quickly. Show visitors that they can do this by using an icon of an upward-pointing arrow, or the words "Back to top", at the bottom of your page.

To create the link, first place the cursor at the top of the page. Click on *Insert* in the Toolbar, and then on *Bookmark...* in the drop-down menu that appears. You will see a window like the one below.

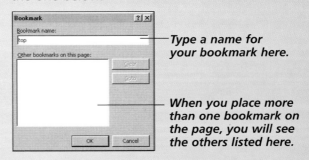

Type a name for your bookmark here.

When you place more than one bookmark on the page, you will see the others listed here.

Give your bookmark a name, then click *OK*. At the top of your page you will now see a little flag symbol (this will not show on the finished page).

Now insert your arrow icon or link words at the bottom of your page. Make them into a hyperlink, as on page 20. In the Insert Hyperlink window, click on the *Bookmark* option.

Click here, then select your bookmark name.

You can place more than one bookmark on a page, if you like. Another neat way of using bookmarks is to have a list of contents at the top of a page, with each item in the list linked to a bookmark further down the page.

Checking your site

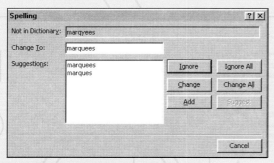

The first part of this book contained a selection of techniques to help you to put together a basic Web site with some fun and interesting features. Once you have put your site together, you are almost ready to publish it on the Internet. Before you do that, though, it's really important to check all the pages thoroughly.

Checking spelling

One check you should always carry out is of the spelling on your pages – a Web site with spelling mistakes looks really sloppy. Microsoft® FrontPage® includes a spell checker, which you'll find under *Tools* in the Menu bar. You may have seen wiggly red underlinings in your text, and corrected any errors already, but it's worth running a final check.

You don't need to highlight text, if you click on *Tools* and then *Spelling...* the spell checker will check all text on the page, highlighting possible errors and suggesting alternatives. When FrontPage finds an unfamiliar word, a window will appear like the one below.

Spelling	? X
Not in Dictionary:	marqyees
Change To:	marquees
Suggestions:	marquees / marques

Ignore | Ignore All
Change | Change All
Add | Suggest
Cancel

FrontPage provides alternatives for unfamiliar words which may be errors.

You can choose to *Ignore* the suggested alternatives (or *Ignore All* if the word appears more than once on the page), select an alternative and *Change* (or *Change All*) if the word is actually wrong, or *Add* the word to FrontPage's dictionary if it is something like a surname that you expect to use again. When the check is complete, you will get a message telling you so.

Using the Preview tab

Page 21 showed you how to use the Preview tab to see how elements would look on your finished page. It's important to check all your pages like this, as there may be slight differences between the look of a page when you are editing it (in the Normal window) and when it is published (as in the Preview window).

You can click on one tab or another at the bottom left-hand corner of your browser window. This makes it easy to go back to the Normal page view if you need to make any changes.

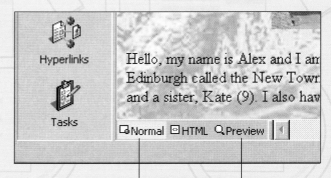

Hyperlinks

Tasks

Hello, my name is Alex and I am Edinburgh called the New Town and a sister, Kate (9). I also hav

Normal | HTML | Preview

You can switch between Normal and Preview windows by clicking on these tabs.

Previewing in your browser

You can also use the Preview in Browser command to view your page. This is particularly useful for checking hyperlinks, as you can simply use your browser's Back and Forward buttons to go quickly from one page to another.

Click on *File* in the Menu bar, and then *Preview in Browser...* from the drop-down menu that appears. A window will appear with your browser's name and a choice of window sizes, related to different screen sizes. Choose *Default* to select your own screen size, or choose a smaller size to make sure your page will still look good. Most screens these days can display Web pages at 800x600, so check your pages at that size if your own screen size is any different.

Checking links

There are other ways of checking the links between pages. You can see a map of the links to and from a particular page by clicking on Hyperlinks in the Views bar on the left of the FrontPage window. You might see something like the map below.

This shows the links to and from a home page.

Plus signs show that there are other pages linked to these ones.

Unbroken blue arrows show working links.

This is a hit counter.

On this map, local links will show as filenames, global links as URLs and mail links as e-mail addresses. Working links will show as straight blue arrows, broken links as broken red arrows. Check and fix any broken links you see.

Downloading time

You may have noticed a little hourglass and a time in seconds at the bottom right-hand corner of the FrontPage window. This tells you approximately how long your page will take to download at various modem speeds. It isn't altogether reliable, but gives you a good idea. Ideally, you want an opening page or a home page to download in under thirty seconds – any longer will be frustrating for your visitors.

If you want to reset the modem speed, click on the time given and select a speed from the list which appears.

Click here to change the modem speed.

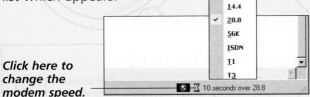

Renaming pages

It may be that once you have created a few pages, you decide it makes sense to rename one or more of them. Don't just rename pages by changing their filenames in the My Webs folder of My Documents, though. Use FrontPage to change the filenames, and all files and links associated with those pages will be updated too.

Click on Folders in the Views bar, and you will see a list like the one below. Click on a page to select it, pause and then click again on the filename (if you click again immediately FrontPage will just open the page). You can now change your filename, and FrontPage will show you a message if there are any links on other pages which need to be updated. Click *OK* to update these links.

This is the Folders list.

Don't delete or rename these two folders. They may be used by FrontPage to store information when your site is published.

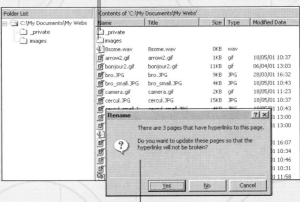

This message appears when links on other pages need updating.

A second opinion

Once your site is ready and you have checked all the links, try asking a friend to give it one last check (do this using the *Preview in Browser...* command, as described on the page opposite, so that they can follow any links easily). They may notice things you have missed, or be able to suggest some improvements.

Ways to publish your site

To publish your site on the Internet, you need to copy it to a server or host computer which will store it and make it available for people to visit. This copying process is called uploading. You can choose between different hosting options.

Servers

A server

Servers are powerful computers which have huge amounts of memory for storing Web sites, and are always switched on so that people can access sites at any time of day, from anywhere in the world. Servers are generally owned and maintained by specialist companies. These companies sell or rent out space to businesses and individuals for their Web sites.

Hosting companies may make use of high-speed connections to the Internet, such as satellite and fibre-optic cable. In theory this means your site should download more quickly; in practice your visitors will see more of a difference if they have a high-speed connection themselves. It's worth visiting the hosting company's home page to see how quickly their own site downloads, but avoid paying extra for high-speed connection services if most of your visitors are unlikely to benefit.

Web space with your ISP

If you have an account with an ISP, your easiest option may be to use the Web space provided by them. Your domain name will be allocated by your ISP; usually it is based on the username you chose when you first signed up. To find out how to upload your site, go to your ISP's Web site and look for instructions in the Members section or the Help section.

The amount of space offered by most ISPs is limited to about 10 or 15 MB, but this should be more than enough for most personal sites. If you find that your site is bigger than that (for example, if it includes a lot of sound clips or animations), you will find more space with a Web-based hosting company. You can check the size of your site in Microsoft® FrontPage® by using the Reports command. (Find out how to do this on page 32.)

These are the logos of ISPs from different countries.

Your own domain name

You can choose and register your own URL ending in .com, .co.uk, .org, .net etc. This is known as domain name registration; your domain name is the name part of your URL, for example Usborne in www.usborne.com. Every URL is unique, so you have to choose a name which has not already been registered by someone else, although you may be able to use the same name with a different ending (www.name.net instead of www.name.com, for example).

Your ISP may offer a domain name registration service, and you often see them advertised in computer magazines. You will have to pay a fee to register the name for a set period (one year, two years, five...), and another fee for hosting your site. Sometimes the registration and hosting fees are combined in the same package.

Web-based hosting

If you build your site on someone else's computer, for example at a library or Internet café, you will need to find a hosting company, or Web Presence Provider, on the Internet. There are a number of Web-based companies that host Web sites free of charge. They generally cover their costs by including advertising on your site. The advertising usually appears as a banner across the top of your page, or a pop-up window which you can close.

Well known Web-based hosting companies include Geocities, now part of the Yahoo!® network, and Angelfire and Tripod, now part of the Lycos® network. Their sites offer help with Web page building, using predesigned templates, but you can also upload a site you have designed yourself.

You will need to sign up as a member to use Web hosting facilities. You can do this quickly and easily on the hosting company's Web site.

These are some popular Web-based hosting companies.

Web hosting services

If you are looking for a Web hosting company, you'll find links to some of the best-known at the Usborne Quicklinks site, **www.usborne-quicklinks.com**

If you want to find a free Web hosting company that supports FrontPage Extensions, try the **Web hosting** page of the **free frontpage stuff** Web site.

You can also find links to **Geocities**, **Tripod**, **Angelfire** and others.

Some hosting companies operate worldwide; others have different pages for the US, the UK and other countries. This means that they can make more domain names available, because the same name can be used with different endings for different countries.

FrontPage Extensions

The easiest way to publish a Web site created with FrontPage is to use the *Publish Web...* command in the *File* menu. To do this, you need to find a Web Presence Provider that supports FrontPage Extensions or has FrontPage Server Extensions installed.

Without FrontPage Server Extensions, some elements on your Web site may not work. This is true of most inserted components, such as hit counters (see page 26) and forms (see pages 42-43). FrontPage Server Extensions also make it easier for you to edit your site using FrontPage at a later date. When you upload your revised files, FrontPage will compare the revised and original versions and update any links as necessary.

You can find a list of Web Presence Providers that support FrontPage Extensions by opening FrontPage and clicking on *File – Publish Web... – WPP's*, which connects you to a page of the Microsoft Web site. Click on Locate an International WPP if you are outside the US or Canada. Most of these companies charge a fee for Web hosting services, but you can find some which are free – see the box on the left.

What if my ISP doesn't support FrontPage Extensions?

You can still upload a site to an ISP without FrontPage Extensions, but you will have to make sure that your site doesn't contain any forms or components such as hit counters. In order to upload your site, you use FTP (File Transfer Protocol). You can find out more about this on page 33.

Uploading your site

Once you have checked your site thoroughly, and decided on a company to host it, you are ready to upload. If your hosting company supports FrontPage Extensions, you can use the *Publish Web...* command. Otherwise you can upload your site using FTP. Both methods are described here.

A final check

Before you publish your page, you should run one last check to be sure that all the links are working, and to see how big the files are. This will tell you how much Web space your site needs.

The best way to do this in Microsoft® FrontPage® is to use the Reports command. Open your home page and click on *View – Reports.* Click on *Site Summary* in the menu that appears. You will see a table like the one below.

This figure shows the size of your site in total.

Site Summary			
Name	Count	Size	Description
All files	56	467KB	All files in the current Web
Pictures	39	414KB	Picture files in the current Web (GIF, JPG, BMP, et
Unlinked files	15	250KB	Files in the current Web that cannot be reached by
Linked files	41	218KB	Files in the current Web that can be reached by st
Slow pages	2	128KB	Pages in the current Web exceeding an estimated
Older files	22	296KB	Files in the current Web that have not been modifi
Recently added fi...	2	3KB	Files in the current Web that have been created in
Hyperlinks	89		All hyperlinks in the current Web
Unverified hyperli...	20		Hyperlinks pointing to unconfirmed target files
Broken hyperlinks	1		Hyperlinks pointing to unavailable target files
External hyperlinks	20		Hyperlinks pointing to files outside of the current V
Internal hyperlinks	69		Hyperlinks pointing to other files within the current
Component errors	2		Files in the current Web with components reporting
Uncompleted tasks	0		Tasks in the current Web that are not yet marked
Unused themes	0		Themes in the current Web that are not applied to

How big is your site?

In the top row, under Size, you will see a figure which tells you the total size of the files on your site. If your site will be hosted by your ISP, check that this is within the limit they have set. For most personal sites, this is not a problem. If your site is over the limit, you may have to edit your site or choose an alternative host.

Slow pages

In the row entitled Slow pages, you will see whether there are any pages which will take longer than 30 seconds to download over a 28K modem. Double-click on this row to see which they are.

Make sure that your home page, at least, doesn't take this long to download. You can edit other pages by including fewer picture files or by creating extra pages and sharing content between them.

You may decide that it doesn't matter if some pages are slow to download. Most people today have modems faster than 28K, but you should still try to limit the number of slow pages as visitors do find them very frustrating.

Hyperlinks

You will see several rows relating to hyperlinks. In the row entitled Unverified hyperlinks, you may see a figure. This means that FrontPage has not tested the link to see that it connects to the right destination. To verify all your hyperlinks, click on *View – Toolbars – Reporting.* You will see a toolbar like the one below. Click on the hyperlink symbol at the right-hand side of this bar. FrontPage will check all your hyperlinks and report any problems.

In the Reports view, you will also see a row entitled Broken hyperlinks. If you run the Verify Hyperlinks check as described above, this should highlight any broken links, which you can then remove or restore.

Click here to verify hyperlinks.

Ready to upload

To upload your site (to a host with FrontPage Server Extensions), first make sure you are online. Then open your home page and click on *File – Publish Web...* You will see a window like the one below.

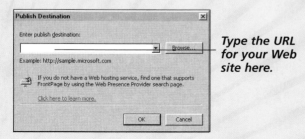

Type the URL for your Web site here.

In the box, type the URL allocated to your Web site by your ISP or hosting company. Then click on *Publish*. You may have to wait a little while for FrontPage to locate your ISP or host.

You will then be asked to give your name and password. This is the username and password you selected when you signed up with your ISP or hosting company.

Type your username here.

FrontPage will then start uploading the pages of your site to your ISP or host. This could also take some minutes. When it is done, you will see a message like the one below. Click on the underlined text to see your published site.

This message tells you your site has been published.

Using FTP

If your host doesn't support FrontPage Server Extensions, you will need to use FTP (File Transfer Protocol) to publish your site. To do this, you will need an FTP client program. Your ISP may offer you a copy, or you can find one easily on the Internet (you can find links to useful Web sites at **www.usborne-quicklinks.com**).

Open your FTP client program. The program used in these examples is called Terrapin FTP. First you need to set up a connection with your ISP's server. Click on *Server – New Connection* and type the server address of your ISP's Web server (your ISP will tell you what this is). Type your username and password, and click on *Connect*.

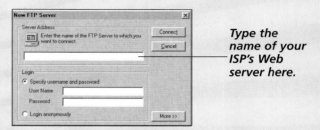

Type the name of your ISP's Web server here.

Once you have established a connection, you will see a window divided into two parts. The top part shows your ISP's server, the bottom part is your own computer. Simply select the files which make up your Web site (remember to select all the image files as well) and drag them into the top window. Your FTP client program will then copy them to your ISP's server.

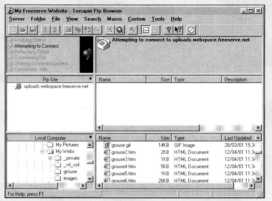

Select and drag files from the bottom window to the top one.

Fan sites

Web sites are a great way for bands, sports teams and movie makers to keep in touch with their fans. You can find some amazing official Web sites, and some unofficial ones which are as good or better. Fans may visit a site once, but the sites have to be really impressive to keep them coming back. They often incorporate sound or video clips – sample tracks on band sites, for instance, or trailers on film sites.

You'll find links to all the sites on this page at **www.usborne-quicklinks.com**

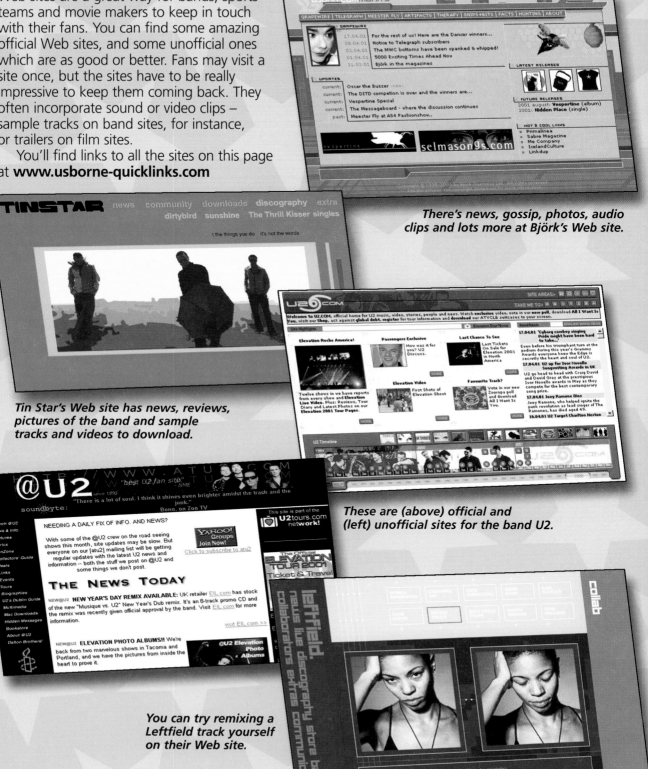

There's news, gossip, photos, audio clips and lots more at Björk's Web site.

Tin Star's Web site has news, reviews, pictures of the band and sample tracks and videos to download.

These are (above) official and (left) unofficial sites for the band U2.

You can try remixing a Leftfield track yourself on their Web site.

The Tomb Raider Movie Web site has lots of pictures, video clips and behind the scenes information.

Catch up with Harry Potter news, watch trailers and look at some other sites created by fans at the official Harry Potter Home Page.

Bayern-München fans can find plenty of news, pictures, discussions and games, in English or German, at the team's Web site.

Find news, statistics and video highlights of Los Angeles Lakers basketball games on the Lakers' Web site.

The Olympique de Marseille site offers video clips of game highlights, playing tips and screensavers, as well as news and pictures of the famous French soccer team.

Preparing sounds

You may like to add sound effects to your Web site. As with pictures, you can either use ready-recorded sounds from collections on the Internet, or incorporate sounds you have recorded yourself.

Finding sound files

Try using a search engine to find sound clips you can use on your site (type in the search terms **free sound effects web site**). Make sure that any sound you plan to use is in the public domain, or copyright-free (see below). You can also find collections of sound effects on CD-ROM.

When you find sound effects on a Web site, they are generally shown as hyperlinks. Click on the link to hear the sound. A program called an audio player will open in a window like the one below. The player shown is Windows Media Player, which is included free with Microsoft® Windows®. Macintosh computers also include audio players which work in a similar way.

Click on these buttons to play, pause or stop the clip.

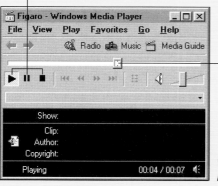

This slider moves across the window as the sound clip plays.

Windows Media Player

To save the sound clip onto your own computer, either follow any instructions given on the site or use your audio player. Click on the clip's hyperlink to open your player, then click on *File* and then *Save As...* Select where you want to store the file on your computer, preferably into My Documents so that you can easily place it on your site, and click *Save*.

Sound file formats

There are various sound file formats, which affect sound quality, file size and whether the files can be played on PCs or Macintosh computers. Whatever format you choose, it's best to keep sound clips fairly short so that your visitors don't have to spend a long time downloading them.

 MP3 files take up very little space but still produce good quality sound. They work on all types of computers.

 AU files can play on all types of computers, but they sometimes sound a bit crackly.

 MIDI files, created with electronic instruments, can play on all computer types and sound better than AU files.

 WAV is the Microsoft Windows audio format. Most browsers can play these files.

 AIFF is the Macintosh audio file format. Most browsers can play these files.

Copyright

If you plan to use sound clips on your Web site, and music in particular, make sure that they are not in copyright. You can find out about copyright on page 8. Music may be the copyright of either the person who wrote it or the artist who performed it, so look out for music or sound clips which are "in the public domain". This means that they are free for anyone to use.

If you use your own music on your site, remember that anyone can access your site and copy sound clips from it, so it is better just to use short extracts.

Recording your own sounds

If you want to record your own sounds for your site, for example a spoken greeting or message, you will need a microphone that you can plug into your computer and a sound editing program.

Windows® 95 and later versions include a basic sound editing program called Sound Recorder. To open it, click on the Start button in the bottom left-hand corner of your screen, then on *Programs – Accessories – Entertainment – Sound Recorder*. You will see a window like the one below.

The Sound Recorder window

You can add an echo, or play your clip backwards if you like, by using the Effects option.

Click on these buttons to play, stop or record clips.

Start recording by clicking on the button with the red circle, and stop by clicking on the button with the black square. When you click on *File – Save As*, Sound Recorder will save the clip in WAV format at "Radio Quality" (medium quality). If you click on *Change...* at the bottom of the Save As window, you can choose "CD Quality" (high) or "Telephone Quality" (low) instead – but remember that the higher quality you choose, the bigger the file will be.

Sound Recorder's Save As window

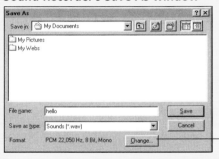

Click here to alter the playing quality.

Converting recorded sounds

If you have a recording that you want to use on your site, for example a band demo, you will need to convert the sound into the right file format. It's easiest if your demo is on a CD and you have a CD-ROM drive on your computer. You will also need a program called an encoder. The encoder used here is called CDex – you can download a free copy via **www.usborne-quicklinks.com**

To convert a track on your CD, place the CD in the CD-ROM drive of your computer and open your encoder. You will see all the tracks on the CD listed. Click on a track to select it, and then select a sound file format.

The CDex encoder window

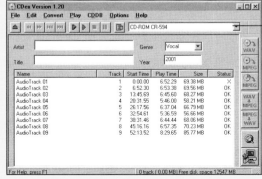

Click here to select a file format.

When you have converted your track, you may like to cut it down a little, to create a shorter extract to place on your site. You can do this by using the Edit command in Sound Recorder.

Open Sound Recorder and play your converted track. If you stop it at a given point, you can delete everything up to that point, or everything after it, until your track is the length you want. Use the Save As command to give your edited track a new name, and save it into My Documents so that you can easily place it on your site.

Sound and video on your Web page

Sound and video files can make your Web site more interactive and fun. You should use them carefully, though, as they take up a lot of Web space and downloading time.

Background sounds

In Microsoft® FrontPage®, you can select a background sound which plays as soon as a Web page opens. Make sure the sound you choose is quite short, preferably only a few seconds' worth, as otherwise your page will take too long to download.

To place the sound, open the page and click *File – Properties...* You will see a window like the one below. (You can also bring up this window by right-clicking anywhere on the page and then clicking on Page Properties in the menu that appears.)

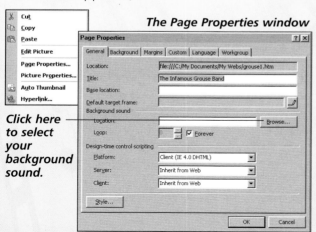

The Page Properties window

Click here to select your background sound.

In the Background sound section, click on *Browse...* to select your sound file. If you want the sound to repeat as long as the page is open, leave the *Forever* box checked, otherwise click to uncheck the box, choose a number of repeats in the *Loop* box, then click *OK*.

Check the downloading time at the bottom right-hand corner of your screen, as on page 28, to make sure that the sound effect won't make your page too slow. Then save the page. You can check that the sound is working by using the Preview tab, as on page 28.

Placing sounds on your page

If you want to use longer sound clips on your Web page, it's best to allow your visitors to choose whether they want to download and listen to them. You can do this by placing sounds as a hyperlink.

Position your cursor on the page and click on the Insert Hyperlink icon in the Toolbar. An Insert Hyperlink window will appear.

Click on this button to locate your sound file, then click on My Documents and find the folder where you have stored your file.

Click on the Browse button to locate your sound file. When you select your file, the filename will appear in the *URL* box of the Create Hyperlink window. Click *OK*, and the filename will appear on your page as a hyperlink. You can test it by using the Preview tab.

Although the hyperlinks themselves won't make your page take any longer to download, the sound files may take a little while, depending on their size. It's a good idea to give the size of each sound file in brackets, to give your visitors an idea of how long they may take.

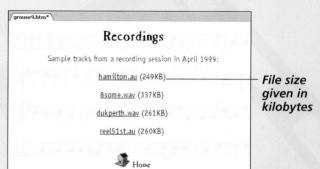

File size given in kilobytes

Video on your page

It's quite easy to insert a video clip using FrontPage, but bear in mind that video takes even more memory space than sound. You should avoid putting video clips on a home page. It's better to have a link to a page containing video, preferably giving some indication of the file size.

You can insert any type of video that can be played by Windows Media Player. When the page downloads, Windows Media Player will download the whole clip and then play it. A few seconds of video can take several minutes to download with a 28.8K modem, so keep clips short and keep an eye on the downloading time at the bottom right-hand corner of your screen.

You insert a video clip in the same way as you insert a picture, as described on page 15. Open the Web page on which you want to place your video, place the cursor on the page and click on *Insert - Picture - Video...* Click on My Documents or the Browse button to locate your video, then click *OK*.

Click on this button to browse for your video file.

You will see the clip as just a black box on your page. To see it playing, you can use the Preview tab at the bottom of the page, as on page 28.

Changing video settings

If you place a video clip as described on the left, it will automatically play once, when the page it appears on is downloaded. You can change the settings so that visitors can choose when to play the clip, or play it more than once. You do this by right-clicking on the clip, and clicking on Picture Properties in the drop-down menu that appears.

The Picture Properties window

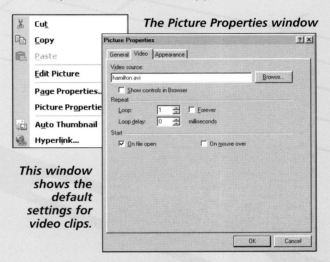

This window shows the default settings for video clips.

If you click on *Show controls in browser*, your visitors will see control buttons underneath the video frame so that they can play and stop the video as they like. (Not all browsers will show these controls, and not all versions of FrontPage offer this option.)

The Repeat settings below this let you choose how many times you want the video to play, and how long a pause you want between play times. You can have the video repeating continuously, if you want! Your visitors' browsers only have to download the file once, so it shouldn't cause the page to take any longer, although it may be a little irritating...

Finally, you can choose whether to have the video play when the page opens, or when your visitors run their mouse over the frame. If you choose the second, it's best to let your visitors know by putting an instruction on the page.

Animation

Animations – moving pictures – are another way of making your page more eye-catching. Short animations need not take a lot of memory, but you should still watch that they don't make your page too slow to download.

GIF animations

GIF animations are made up of a series of GIF files (see page 23) played continuously one after the other. Because GIF files themselves are fairly small, the animations can generally be downloaded quickly and without problems. You can find GIF animations easily on the Internet – they are often included in clip art collections (see page 14). You'll find a link to one useful site at **www.usborne-quicklinks.com**, or try a search engine (type in the search terms **free gif animation**).

Placing GIF animations

Once you have found a GIF animation that you want to use, and saved a copy onto your own computer, you place it on a Web page in the same way that you place any image in Microsoft® FrontPage®. Position the cursor on the page and click on *Insert – Picture – From File...*, then locate your animation file.

Find your animation file in My Pictures or My Documents.

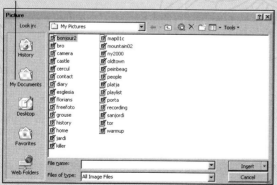

Click *OK*. The animation will appear on your page as an ordinary still picture, but you can see it working by clicking on the Preview tab, as on page 28.

Sketch your animation on paper first.

Create your own animation

You can create your own animated GIF using a program called a GIF animator. You can find a number of GIF animators on the Internet – they are not very expensive, and many are available in a free trial version. You'll find a link to one easy-to-use trial at **www.usborne-quicklinks.com**

Before you start, plan your animation on paper. Keep it quite short, to keep the file size down – ideally don't use more than 12 frames. Next, create your images using your graphics program, or scan in images on paper. Save the files as GIFs, and give each file a name that tells you where it comes in the animation sequence (anim1.gif, anim2.gif and so on).

When all the individual files are ready, open your GIF animator and place all the files in sequence. You can set the animation to "loop" (repeat continuously) or to repeat a set number of times. Save your completed animation. Your GIF animator will save it to take up as little file space as possible. You can then place it on your Web page.

These four images make up a flying bird animation.

Java™

Another kind of animation is created using a programming language called Java. Java is used to write mini-programs called "applets" which can then be placed on a Web page. Java applets can animate images, play sounds or change the appearance of elements on a Web page when you run your mouse over them. The picture on the right, for example, looks as though it is under rippling water.

This Java applet makes the picture look as though it is under water when you run your mouse over it.

Collections of Java applets are also easy to find on the Internet. Some sites are listed below.

It's quite tricky to place a Java applet using FrontPage (although relatively easy using HTML, and most Java sites explain the procedure for HTML). You will need to download the applet to your own computer, but also to link back to the site where you found it, so keep a note of this.

In FrontPage, position the cursor on your page and click *Insert – Web Component... – Advanced Controls – Java Applet*. A window will appear like the one below. Fill in the applet's filename (Java filenames usually end in .class) and the URL of the site where you found it.

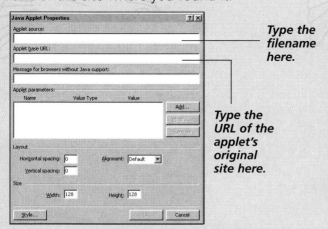

Type the filename here.

Type the URL of the applet's original site here.

There is also space for you to type a message for browsers which don't support Java – some older versions of browsers don't automatically run Java applets. Then there is a large box for "Applet

parameters" – you should find details of these on the site where you found the applet. Add all the parameters specified. In the Layout section, you can select the applet's position on the page and its size. Finally click *OK*, and save your page. You can then see the applet working by using the Preview tab.

Flash™

Many commercial sites use a kind of animation called Flash. Flash produces spectacular animation effects that download quickly and play smoothly. You need a special player to view Flash sites, but you can download this easily from **www.macromedia.com**.

Flash isn't quite like GIF animations or Java, in that you won't find many free-to-use collections of animations on the Internet. It is also tricky to use in FrontPage (you would place it as a plug-in, clicking *Insert – Advanced – Plug-in...*, but the Flash code itself may need some adjusting for the animation to work). However, if you are seriously interested in animation for Web pages, you can find how to download a free trial version and tutorials on page 55 of this book.

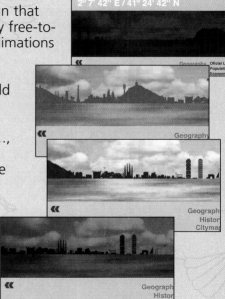

In this Flash animation the camera pans around the harbour and night turns to day as you watch.

Animations for your site

Go to **www.usborne-quicklinks.com** for links to great animation sites such as **2Cool Animations** (GIF animations) and **Java Boutique** (Java applets)

Collecting information

If you want to find out more about your visitors, you can create a form on your Web site to gather details. Forms can be used to ask for feedback or take membership details for clubs or societies. They can also take personal and financial details on a commercial Web site – many of the processes involved are the same.

Forms are easy to place in Microsoft® FrontPage®, although they are FrontPage components, so you need to make sure your Web hosting company supports FrontPage Extensions (see page 31).

Placing a form on a page

In FrontPage, you create a basic form on a Web page by positioning your cursor on the page and clicking *Insert – Form – Form*. On your page, you will see a rectangle with a dotted outline, like the one below. (The dotted line will not appear on the finished page.)

You add elements to this form to collect different kinds of information.

Almost all forms on the Internet contain Submit and Reset buttons, so these are included automatically in the FrontPage form. Your visitors will click on Submit to send the completed form to you, and Reset to clear the form if they want to make changes to the details they have given.

Now you can add boxes to your form to collect different kinds of information.*

Names and addresses

FrontPage allows you to collect information in various different ways. For example, if you want to know someone's name and e-mail address, you can just give them a short text box in which they can type the information you need.

First type what it is you're asking for. This is known as a prompt (for example, "Your name:"). Then click on *Insert – Form – Textbox*, and click Return. You can do this for as many entries as you like.

Use one-line text boxes for visitors to type in short items, such as e-mail addresses.

Radio buttons

Radio buttons, or option buttons, allow visitors to choose one of several options, for example a particular age range. You can click on any item in a list, but only one item can be selected at a time.

Type your list of prompts, and after each item in the list click on *Insert – Form – Option button* After each prompt, click Tab or Return to separate the items so that it is clear which button belongs to which item. For each group of prompts with radio buttons, FrontPage will only allow one button to be selected at a time.

Radio buttons allow visitors to select just one option.

*Under the 1998 Data Protection Act in the UK, you may collect "personal data" such as names and e-mail addresses for your own personal, recreational use only. If you are using the data for any other purposes you should refer to the Office of the Information Commissioner. Find out more at www.dataprotection.gov.uk

Check boxes

Radio buttons only allow visitors to select one option, and one option must always be selected. However, you may want to allow several items in a list to be selected – in a list of hobbies, for example. You may also want an option which can be left unselected – if you are offering to send someone information, maybe. You can do this by using check boxes.

Type your prompt or prompts, as for radio buttons. After each one, click *Insert – Form – Checkbox*. Visitors can click on the box to select it, and click again to clear it.

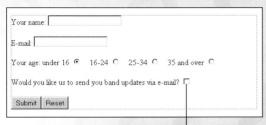

Visitors can choose whether to select this option or not.

Scrolling text boxes

If you want to give visitors more than one line space to type text – for example, if you are asking for their comments – you can insert a text box which gives them as much room as they need. Type your prompt, then click *Insert – Form – Text Area* (or *Scrolling Text Box*). The box that appears on the page is quite small, but if you click on it you will see eight black points around the edges, and you can drag any of these points to make the box wider or longer.

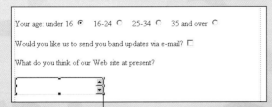

Click and drag these points to expand your text box if you want.

Processing the information

Once you have finished your form, save your page. You can format the form as you would any other text – changing the font, size, position of items and so on. You can see how it will look on the finished page by using the Preview tab, as on page 28.

Now you need to arrange for information you collect to be processed and sent back to you. You will only be sent whatever your visitors type on the page, so in order to make sense of the results, it helps to give a name to each entry, or form field.

To do this, right-click on a form field, for example the one-line text box next to "Your name:". In the menu that appears, click on *Form Field Properties...* The *Name:* box has the default name T1, but it makes sense to change this to "Name". Click *OK*. Then do the same for the box next to "E-mail:", naming it "E-mail", and so on.

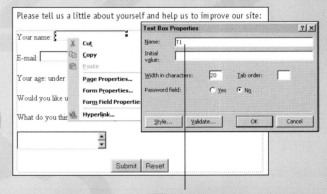

Give a name to each form field. Radio buttons have a group name: give the same name to each button in the group.

Finally, you can arrange for the results to be sent to you. FrontPage includes a device called a form handler which automatically sends results to a file in the _private folder of your Web structure. However, it may be more convenient for you to receive results via e-mail. To do this, right-click anywhere on the form and click on *Form properties*. In the window that appears, type your e-mail address in the box next to *E-mail address:*, then click *OK*.

Using tables

Tables are a really useful way of presenting a lot of information clearly on a Web page. They can also be used to set up the page itself – although you may not see them, tables form the structure for many well-designed Web pages.

Inserting a table

To place a table on a page in Microsoft® FrontPage®, position your cursor and click *Table* – *Insert* – *Table*... You will see a window like the one below.

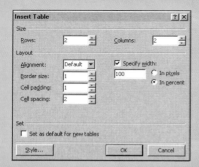

Use this window to define your table size and the number of rows and columns.

Decide how many rows (horizontal) and columns (vertical) you want your table to have. Unless you change the default settings, your table will cover the full width of your Web page (but you can set a different width, either as a percentage of your page or as a fixed width measured in pixels). It will have a narrow border around and between the rows and columns, but you can make this invisible by changing the border width to 0.

Now you can begin to fill in your table. Each space in the table is called a cell, and you can treat each cell differently, changing the position and appearance of text and changing the background colour. Use the standard formatting toolbar at the top of the FrontPage window to change the font and size, make text bold or centre it. Use the tab key and the arrow keys to jump from one cell to another, or simply reposition the cursor in a different cell. You can also use your mouse cursor to highlight items in one cell and drag them into another.

Using the table tools

If you click on *View* – *Toolbars* – *Tables*, you will see a toolbar like the one below. The icons represent some useful ways of editing your table.

Click on these symbols to add rows or columns.

Click here to delete cells.

Click here to merge cells or to subdivide them.

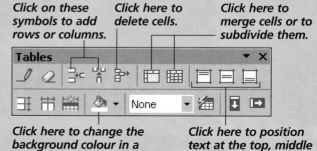

Click here to change the background colour in a selected cell or cells.

Click here to position text at the top, middle or bottom of a cell.

The table below uses a few of these effects.

These cells have a different background colour.

The text in these cells has been positioned at the top of the cell.

BAND BOOKINGS 2001

Date	Start time	Venue
26 January	9.45pm	Hammersmith Town Hall, London
2 February	10.0pm	Fulham Town Hall, London
24 February	9.30pm	Thistle Grand Hotel, Bristol
17 March	9.0pm	Fulham Town Hall, London
28 April	9.0pm	Les Fauxquets, Guernsey
26 May	9.0pm	Gathering Hall, Portree
14 July	9.45pm	Moor Park, Shropshire
22 September	9.0pm	Forthampton Court, Gloucestershire
24 November	9.30pm	Guildhall, Bath
TBC	9.30pm	Cercul Militar, Bucharest

These two columns were created by splitting one wider column.

To edit a cell or a group of cells (they must be in the same row or column), use your cursor to highlight them and then click on the appropriate icon in the Tables toolbar. To merge two cells, for example, highlight both cells and click on the Merge Cells icon in the Tables toolbar.

If you want to change the column width or the row height, move your cursor over the border between rows or columns. You will see that it changes to a double-headed arrow. You can then drag the border to the width or height you want, so long as there is room in the cells of that row or column for any text you have placed in them.

Placing pictures in a table

As well as text, you can include pictures in a table. Simply position your cursor in the cell where you want the picture and then click on *Insert – Picture* as you would to place a picture on the page normally.

The cell will expand to fit the picture, so you may want to shrink or crop it a little. Page 15 tells you how to shrink an image by dragging the corner points. To crop it (that is, cut away the part you don't need), click on the image to select it and then click on the cropping tool in the Pictures toolbar. You will see a dotted line around your image, with eight points around it. Click and drag the points until the dotted line encloses the area you want, then click on the cropping tool again.

Click and drag these points to select the area you want.

This is the cropping tool.

Transparent backgrounds

Another useful picture tool for tables is the transparent colour wand, which appears to the right of the cropping tool. If you are placing a logo in a table, you might find that it includes a white background that you would prefer to remove. Select the picture and click on the transparent colour tool. Your cursor will turn into a wand image when it is over a picture. Touch an area of one colour, such as the background, to make it transparent.

Using tables to design a page

You can use all these techniques when you base a page design on a table. The table structure allows you to give page headings, links, images and blocks of text their own areas on a page. You can have several blocks of text side by side, perhaps as "taster" pieces with links to pages where you have more information. You can fit a lot of information on a page in this way, without it becoming messy and confusing. At the same time, the table can adapt to different screen sizes so that your page appears in proportion and looks good.

When you set up your table, set the border size to 0. You'll see the borders as dotted lines in the Normal view when you are designing the page, so that you can see where the cells are. These won't show, though, when you use the Preview tab or when you publish your page.

On the page below, the dotted lines show the cell borders.

This cell contains links to other pages. **This cell contains the page title.** **This cell contains a "special events" banner.**

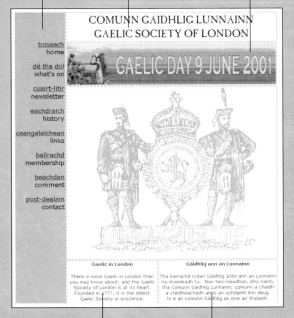

These two cells make it possible to show text in two languages. The Gaelic text is slightly longer than the English, so the cell on the right is slightly wider.

Maintaining and updating your site

Once your site is published, it's important to review it regularly and keep it up to date. You may have additions or improvements to make, or you may find that some of your links break down and need updating or replacing.

Checking your site

Use your own and other computers to visit your site from time to time. You may find that the site looks different when viewed using a different computer, screen size or browser – for example, colours on a Macintosh computer appear brighter than on a PC. Ask other people's opinions, too.

Perhaps the most important details to check for are broken links and pages that are slow to download. Both of these are very frustrating for visitors, so try to fix them quickly. You can either check these by visiting your page or by using the Reports command, as described on page 32.

Adding a date

If you plan to update your site regularly, it's a good idea to make a feature of the date so that your visitors can see just how current the page is. Using Microsoft® FrontPage®, you can easily add a line of text at the bottom of your home page, then insert the date by clicking on *Insert – Date and Time...* Each time you go back to edit the page, this line will be updated.

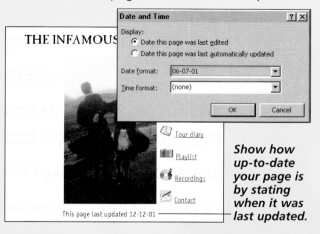

Show how up-to-date your page is by stating when it was last updated.

Deleting unwanted files

When you've worked on your site a little, you may find that the Site Summary (see page 32) includes files you no longer plan to use. These may be images you have since replaced, or components you have decided not to have on the site.

If you want to get rid of them altogether, use the Reports view to list them – click on *View – Reports – All Files*. Click on the file or files to select them, then press Delete. You will get a message asking whether you are sure you want to delete. Click on *Yes* if you are sure.

The file and all links to it will be deleted, so make sure you check for broken hyperlinks (see page 32) before you upload your updated site.

Files you don't want to publish

If you don't want to delete files altogether, save them in FrontPage but mark them as not to be published. You can then use them again in later versions of your site if you want.
Click on *View – Reports – Workflow – Publish Status*. You will see a list of files similar to the *All Files* list. Right-click on a file and then click on *Don't Publish*. (In older versions of FrontPage, click on *Properties...* and then click on the Workgroup tab; click in the box next to *Exclude this file when publishing the rest of the Web*, then click *OK*.)

The red cross symbol shows you that the file will not be uploaded when you come to update your site.

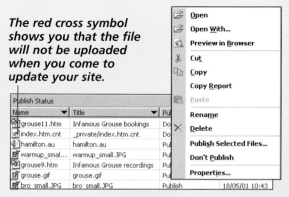

The file will be saved, but will not be uploaded to your Web server.

Updating your site

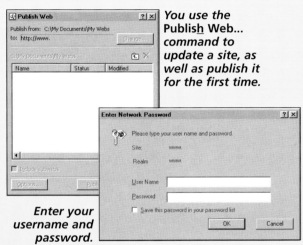

If you use the *Publish Web...* command in FrontPage to upload your site, it's easy to make changes and publish the latest version. Open a page of your site and click on *File – Publish Web...* You will see a window like the one below, with your site's URL already filled in.

You use the Publish Web... command to update a site, as well as publish it for the first time.

Enter your username and password.

You will be asked to give your username and password, as you did when you first published the site (see page 33). FrontPage will then compare the version of your site on your own computer with the version on your hosting company's server, and upload any updated pages. When the uploading process is complete, you will get a message to tell you so. However, it may take a day before you can view your updated site on the Internet.

Updating your site using FTP

If you used FTP to upload your site, as described on page 33, all you have to do is to open your FTP client program and wait until it has established a connection with your ISP or Web server. Then drag your updated files from the bottom part of the FTP client program window (representing your computer) to the top (representing your ISP). Your FTP client will automatically replace the older files with your updated versions.

Publicizing your site

When you are satisfied with your site, you'll want to encourage people to visit. Start by telling friends about the site – you can send them the URL in an e-mail.

To make your site more widely known, the best approach is to submit it to one or more search engines. Yahoo!®, for example, has a special category for personal home pages. You'll find a list of search engines in the box below.

Most search engines have a form you can use to tell them about your site. Their staff will then generally check your site before listing it (the check may take a few weeks, as so many new Web sites are created every day). Alternatively, you can use a service that automatically submits your site to a number of search engines.

To submit a site to Yahoo!, use the directory to go to the category you think is most suitable for your site, for example **Society and Culture – People – Personal Home Pages**. Click on "Suggest a Site" at the bottom of the page, and you will be taken through a simple four-step submission procedure, in which you give details of your site, a brief description and your own contact details. Once submitted, your site will be checked and then listed in the directory.

Search engines

Go to **www.usborne-quicklinks.com** for links to some of the most popular search engines, such as **Yahoo!**®, **Lycos**® and **Google**SM.

Some of these have different search engines for different countries, so choose whether you want to submit to the main US-based site or to the sites for the UK or other countries.

You'll also find links to the **AddMe** and **Submit Express** Web sites, which offer services including submitting sites free of charge to a range of search engines.

Organizations and businesses

Large organizations have the means to produce some really impressive Web sites, which can be an important way for them to promote and sell their products. It's fun to see what can be done with plenty of time and resources. Different kinds of sites have different styles – it's best for a fashion site to be fun and colourful, for example, while a travel site should be streamlined and easy to use.

You'll find links to all the sites on this page at **www.usborne-quicklinks.com**

An elegant site from Céline, the French fashion house, showing details of its collections

Paul Frank has a fun animated site featuring fashions and homeware.

Online bookstores such as amazon.com have lots of "tasters" of different kinds of books and music on their home pages. There are dozens of links to pages where you can find out more, or find similar titles.

This Spanish online share-dealing service presents complex financial information clearly.

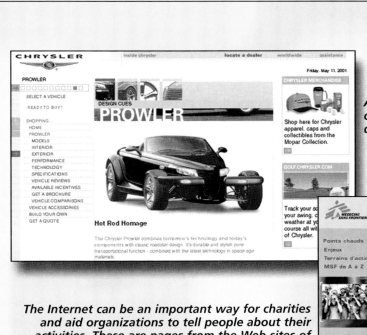

At Chrysler's Web site you can "build your own" dream car online.

The Internet can be an important way for charities and aid organizations to tell people about their activities. These are pages from the Web sites of Médecins Sans Frontières and Unicef.

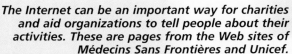

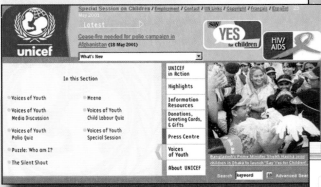

Apple's Web site sets out to be well-designed and easy to use, like its computers.

Nike's many international sites have a huge collection of sporting facts, playing tips and fun downloads, as well as selling Nike products

Special features on commercial sites

Web sites that sell products or services need to incorporate extra features to help customers find and buy the products they want. These include efficient search facilities and secure methods of payment. Many sites also include advertising to highlight products or special offers.

Contact details

If you want to set up a commercial Web site, it's important to let customers know how to contact you. People are concerned about paying for goods on the Internet, so any selling site needs to reassure its customers as much as possible. Many commercial sites list business addresses, phone and fax numbers and e-mail addresses at the bottom of their home pages, or have a contact link on all pages to another page which has this information. It's helpful for visitors to know that the organization has a "real" base. They may also need this information if there is any problem with their orders.

Search forms

Search forms are essential on sites that offer a lot of information or a large range of products. They can be tailored to suit visitors' needs – for example, an online bookstore might allow you to search the entire site or narrow your search down by searching a particular category. Other stores might let you search for items within a particular price bracket.

Search forms for an online bookstore, a newspaper archive and a property agent.

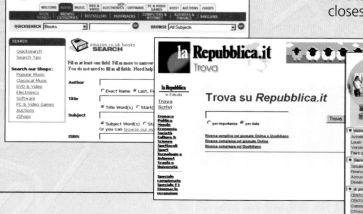

Placing a search form

You can include a simple search form in a site created using some versions of Microsoft® FrontPage®, although as a FrontPage component it will only work if your Web hosting company supports FrontPage Extensions (see page 31). You can place your form on a single page, generally your home page, but it will actually search all the pages on your site.

To place a search form, first open your page and position your cursor, then click *Insert – Component – Search form...* You will see a window like the one below.

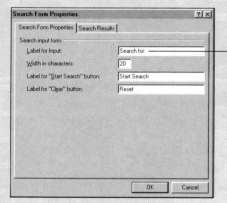

These are the default settings. You can change them if you like.

FrontPage has default settings for the search prompt (*Label for Input:*), the width of the input box and so on, but you can alter these if you like. Click *OK* to place your form. You can preview it using the Preview tab, but you won't be able to test it until you publish the page.

When you do try a search, type in one or more words to search for. The search results will appear as a list of links, with the best matches at the top of the list (those which feature most of the words you specified, or feature them closest together).

Secure payment

Customers are worried that, if they give their credit card details on a Web site, the details may be intercepted by fraudsters who can then use them to run up huge bills.

Credit card fraud of this kind is quite rare, but companies can best protect themselves and their customers by using a system called Secure Sockets Layer (SSL). This makes it possible to encrypt customers' credit card details, so that they can only be read by the Web server to which they are being sent.

SSL makes it possible to set up secure pages on a Web site. Some browsers show a message advising visitors when they are using a secure connection, meaning that any information they send will be encrypted. Visitors can also tell a secure connection by the locked padlock symbol that appears at the bottom of the browser window, and by the fact that the page's URL begins with **https://** instead of **http://**

This prefix and symbol indicate a secure server.

If you need to use SSL for a site created using FrontPage, it's best to contact your Web hosting company and ask their advice. When you come to upload the site, there is a check box in the Publish Web window. This allows you to select *Secure connection required (SSL)* if you need it.

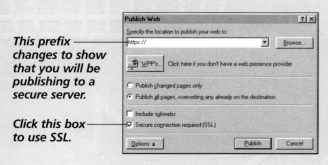

This prefix changes to show that you will be publishing to a secure server.

Click this box to use SSL.

Advertising

Commercial sites can use advertising in different ways. Many use "banner" advertising across the top of their pages to draw visitors' attention to particular products or offers. Banners often use animation or alternating text to make them more eye-catching. You click on the banner to find out more about the product in question. Pop-up windows work in a similar way – a small window appears in the top left-hand corner of the screen, and you click to enlarge it and find out more, or to close it if you aren't interested.

Companies can also advertise on other people's sites. This may be quite expensive, especially on popular sites such as search engines, so some companies operate a system of "banner exchange," and advertise on each other's sites.

Advertising on a personal site

Individuals as well as companies can have advertising on their sites (indeed, if your site is hosted by a Web-based company such as Geocities, the company will cover its costs by showing some advertising on your site). A number of companies offer payment for ads on your site – generally you receive a small payment if your visitor clicks on the ad, or gives their details to the advertising company.

Although the idea of making money from your Web site is tempting, you should think about it carefully. Some visitors find banners and pop-up ads distracting and annoying. It's estimated that fewer than one in a hundred visitors actually click on a banner, so unless you have a large number of visitors, you are unlikely to make much money. If you do include ads on your site, choose them carefully – visitors are much more likely to click on ads that are relevant to the site's content.

Banner ads can be irritating...

HEY! LOOK AT ME!

Using HTML

Web editors such as Microsoft® FrontPage® make page design easy, because you can see exactly what effect you are creating on a page. To build on your Web design skills, though, you need to understand a little about HTML, the basic language of all Web editors and all Web design. Don't panic – it's not as hard as it looks. These two pages will get you started.

Tags

HTML is basically a set of instructions which tell a browser what to show on a Web page and how to show it. These may include text size, colour, style and position, images, sounds, animations and, most importantly, hyperlinks. HTML can be used to build up a really complicated page, but HTML files themselves take up hardly any space and can be read and processed by a browser incredibly quickly.

HTML instructions are called tags, and almost always come in pairs, like quotation marks, opening and closing. Opening tags are in angular brackets <like this>, and closing ones in angular brackets with a slash </like this>. If you open a page in FrontPage and click on the HTML tab at the bottom of the window, you will see the tags: they appear in blue, with the actual instructions in black.

This is the HTML code for the beginning of a page designed in FrontPage.

```
index.htm                                              ×
<html>

<head>
<meta http-equiv="Content-Language" content="en-gb">
<meta http-equiv="Content-Type" content="text/html; charset=windows-1252">
<meta name="GENERATOR" content="Microsoft FrontPage 4.0">
<meta name="ProgId" content="FrontPage.Editor.Document">
<title>toiseach</title>
<meta name="Microsoft Border" content="none">
</head>

<body>

<table border="0" height="170" cellpadding="3" width="737">
  <tr>
    <td height="614" rowspan="5" bgcolor="#99CCFF" valign="top" width="117">
      <p align="right"><br>
Normal  HTML  Preview
```

Try designing a basic page in HTML yourself. Start by opening a basic text editing program such as Notepad on a PC (or SimpleText on a Macintosh computer).

Head and body

Every Web page has two parts: the "head", which contains information about the page, such as its title, and the "body", which contains what actually appears on the page in a browser. For your basic page, you need to start by telling the browser that the page is written in HTML. Then give the page a head, with a title (this will only appear in the browser's title bar, but it is important for identifying the page). Then close the head and open the body of the page, as below.

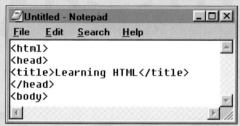

```
Untitled - Notepad                        _ □ ×
File   Edit   Search   Help
<html>
<head>
<title>Learning HTML</title>
</head>
<body>
```

Notice the opening and closing tags.

Heading and main text

Next, give your page a heading. All your text will align to the left unless you tell the browser otherwise, so you can centre your heading with the tag `<center>`. Then choose a size, from h1 (largest) to h6 (smallest). Sizes h1-h3 are usual for headings. Remember to close the tags.

Next, choose a size for your main text, from 1 (smallest) to 7 (largest) – you can check the sizes on page 12 of this book. Type some text. If you type more than one paragraph, separate the paragraphs using the tag `<p>`. You don't need to close this tag as it can work as a complete instruction in itself, known as a standalone tag.

```
<body>
<center>
<h2>Using HTML</h2>
</center>
<font size=4>Web editors such as Microsoft®
FrontPage®  make page design easy, because
you can see exactly what effect you are
creating on a page.
<p>
To build on your Web design skills, though,
you need to understand a little about HTML,
the basic language of all Web editors and
all Web design. Don't panic – it's not as
hard as it looks. </font>
```

Saving and viewing your page

To see what you have done so far, finish your document with the tags `</body>` and `</html>` Then save your page into My Documents, giving it a name ending in **.htm** or **.html**

Open your My Documents folder and double-click on your file. Your browser will open onto your page.

Double-click on your file...

...to view it in your browser.

Colour

You can easily add colour to either the text or the background of your page. All colours are based on the primary colours red, green and blue, and are defined by six-figure codes. Some useful colour codes are shown below.

To colour the background of your page, include the colour code in the Body tag. For a pale blue background, use the tag `<body bgcolor= #CCCCFF>`, for example. You don't need to close the colour tag separately; it's enough to close the Body tag in the usual way: `</body>`

To colour the text, add a Font Color tag after the heading size or the font size. `<font color= #000088>` will give you a dark blue. You can change colours within a piece of text simply by inserting a new Font Color tag. Again, you only need to close the Font tag `</font>` at the end.

Images

To include an image in an HTML document, you need to state its file name so that the browser can locate and download it. For a background image which will be tiled across a whole page, include its file name in the Body tag: `<body background="mountain02.gif">`

For a foreground image, you need also to give the image size, either in pixels or as a percentage of the page size. You may also want to centre it on the page. To produce the home page on page 17 of this book, for example, you would start the body with the following code:

```
<body background="mountain02.jpg">
<center>
<h2><b>Welcome! Bienvenue! Willkommen!</b></h2>
<img src="edincastle2.jpg" width="380">
<br>
<font size=2>Edinburgh Castle, by Ian Britton,<br>
at <u>www.freefoto.com</u></font>
```

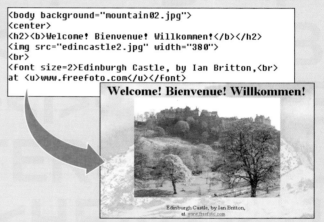

Links

To place a hyperlink on a page, whether local or remote, you use a tag called an anchor tag. This tells the browser to go to another page, and tells it where that page is located. To make the URL on the page above into a hyperlink, you would use the anchor tag `<a href="http://www.freefoto.com">` and then give the URL as you want it to appear on the page. Close the tag with `</a>`

If you are linking to another page of your own site, you don't need to give the full address but only the file name of the linked page, ending in **.htm** or **.html** All the pages of a site will be stored on the same server, so browsers will be able to find linked pages easily.

#FFFFFF   #FFFF00   #FF0000   #880000   #00FFFF   #00FF00   #008800   #FF00FF   #0000FF   #000088   #000000

Going further

Microsoft® FrontPage® is a good way to get started with Web design, and it's essential to know a little about HTML in order to see how site building works. Once you are comfortable with basic site design, though, you might like to try out some more advanced Web design packages, such as Macromedia® Dreamweaver®.

What is Dreamweaver?

Dreamweaver is a powerful Web design program which allows you to lay out a page using a table structure and add elements such as Flash™ animations and interactive features. You can see some of the amazing sites created with Dreamweaver on Macromedia's showcase site (see page 59).

Dreamweaver is fairly expensive to buy, but you can download a free 30-day trial version from Macromedia – find a link to the trial version at **www.usborne-quicklinks.com**. Macromedia also produce a useful tutorial, which takes 1-2 hours to complete and gives you an excellent idea of how the program works. You can download a printable version via the Usborne Quicklinks Web site.

Use Dreamweaver to build a table, then place text and images in it, Flash effects and more. The links on this page use a "rollover" effect: they change colour when the mouse cursor runs over them.

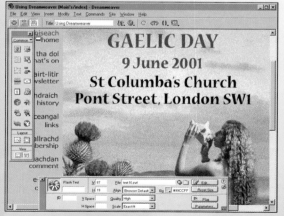

The text headings have been converted into graphics, which means that they will not change on computers which don't have the same fonts.

Flash™ animation

Flash animation has a number of advantages over other forms of animation used on Web pages. If you have seen Flash animations, you may have noticed that they are smoother and sharper than other kinds. This is because they use "vector graphics", in which lines and shapes are defined by mathematical formulae, rather than pixel by pixel as in other graphics files. The formulae take up much less memory, so the files download quickly.

Flash animations can be much easier to produce than, for example, GIF animations. For a GIF animation (see page 40) you need to provide every frame in the animation. With Flash, you can use a process called "tweening": you provide the beginning and end of a sequence, and tell Flash to create the steps in between. You can use tweening to move an object across a screen, fade it in and out, rotate it or change its shape, size or colour.

Flash, too, is expensive to buy, but you can download a free 30-day trail version from the Macromedia Web site – you'll find a link at **www.usborne-quicklinks.com** When you open Flash, you'll find some excellent tutorials to show you around its tools and techniques under *Help – Lessons*.

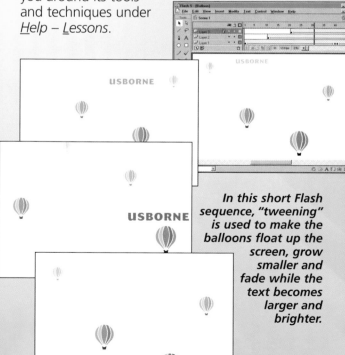

In this short Flash sequence, "tweening" is used to make the balloons float up the screen, grow smaller and fade while the text becomes larger and brighter.

Obtaining Web design software

You can obtain trial copies of many excellent Web design programs. Generally trial copies work for a limited period – 30, 45 or 60 days – after which you can decide whether you want to buy the full version. It's also worth looking out for computer magazines offering Web design software – many magazines include CDs with free software which may be useful to you.

Microsoft® FrontPage®

In certain countries, you can order a trial copy of FrontPage 2002 from Microsoft – you'll find details at **www.usborne-quicklinks.com**. The full version is not too expensive to buy – you may find either FrontPage 2000 or FrontPage 2002, which has a few more features.

Macromedia products

You can find 30-day trial versions of both Macromedia® Dreamweaver® and Flash™ on the Macromedia Web site. You'll find links to the trial offers for both programs at **www.usborne-quicklinks.com**.

You can choose to pay for a full copy at any point during your trial period: each time you open up the program, you can click on *Try* (to continue using the trial version) or *Buy Now*. If you choose *Buy Now*, a form will appear for you to fill in with your credit card details, so that you can pay for your copy online.

Online resources

You'll find a wealth of Web sites with tips, tutorials and material you can use on your own site. (Always check that it is not in copyright though – see pages 8 and 36). You'll find links to the following, and other useful sites, on the Usborne Quicklinks Web site at **www.usborne-quicklinks.com**

reallybig.com Links to thousands of sites offering clip art collections, Java applets, HTML tutorials and more.

free frontpage stuff Links to several good tutorial sites, as well as to a number of free Web Presence Providers which support FrontPage Extensions.

Thomas Brunt's Outfront Hundreds of tips for page building with FrontPage, including easy-to-follow "viewlets", animations of common FrontPage tasks. The techniques page is particularly helpful.

Webmonkey A huge library of tutorials and tips for Web page design using HTML. There's also a special kids' site which makes basic HTML fun and easy to understand.

Webgenies Aimed mainly at younger children, another great collection of tutorials, tips and links to other resources sites.

Flash Kit Tutorials A collection of general tutorials and help with specific features of Flash, at all levels.

If you have a specific problem with your Web site, try typing keywords into a search engine to see if anyone has produced an advice page or help page for your question. A good search engine to try is **Google**.

What makes a great Web site?

Almost anyone can build a Web site, but really well-designed sites are relatively rare. Even large organizations with lots of design resources can produce boring or even irritating sites. On these two pages you'll find tips to help you produce a site that looks good and works well.

Backgrounds

It's very tempting to choose from the huge range of patterned backgrounds to be found on the Internet. Backgrounds are easy to place and seem more fun than plain white pages. Choose very carefully, though, as a pattern which looks great in a small sample can be overpowering when tiled across a whole page.

If you do use a background, make sure your text is still clearly readable – if you aren't sure yourself, preview your page in a browser (see page 28) and ask a friend's opinion.

Colour

Use colours much more carefully than you would on paper – clashing colours can be particularly irritating on screen. At the same time, make sure that the text colour contrasts well with the background so that the text is easy to read.

Some colours work particularly well on Web sites, especially muted versions of the base colours red, green and blue. Try using shades of the same colour, with possibly one other colour to contrast (and black and white as needed). Any more than this may start to look fussy.

Shades in the same colour group look best.

Images

Always bear downloading time in mind when you include images or animations on a page. Try to use images in a low-resolution format that doesn't take up a lot of file space. Use just a few images on a page, or use thumbnail versions (see page 25) that link to larger pictures.

In case your visitors have any problems downloading an image, or can't view an animation, you can include "alternative text". This appears as a label below your mouse cursor when the cursor is over the picture area. If the picture fails to download, at least your visitors can see what's missing. This is especially useful if the picture is itself a hyperlink – your alternative text can tell visitors, "Click here to see" the linked page.

To place alternative text in Microsoft® FrontPage®, right-click on a picture and click *Picture Properties...* In the General section of the window, in the box beside *Text,* type a caption to your picture and then click *OK.* You can see the effect by using the Preview tab, as on page 28.

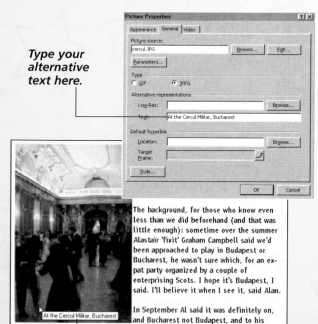

Type your alternative text here.

Your alternative text appears when you let your cursor rest on an image

Navigation

Be sure to make your site easy for your visitors to find their way around. Include a link back to the home page on every page – in time, you may have visitors arriving at pages of your site other than the home page. "Back" and "Forward" (or "Previous" and "Next") links are also useful, as well as "Back to top" and other bookmarks in a long piece of text (see page 27).

If your site is quite extensive, you might think about having a navigation bar across the top or on the left of the page. This is a section with links to all the main pages of your site, and it appears consistently on every page to make it easy for visitors to get around the site.

To place a navigation bar in FrontPage, open a page of your site and click *Insert – Navigation...* In the latest versions of FrontPage, you choose from several link bar options; the most helpful might be *Bar based on navigation structure*.

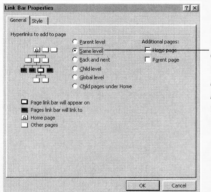

Choose which level of pages you want the navigation bar to link with.

Next, choose which pages you want the navigation bar to link to – "parent" or "child" level (the pages above or below the one you have selected in the navigation structure), same level, back and next, etc., then click *OK*.

The links in the navigation bar will use the titles you have given your pages (see page 11) as they appear in your navigation structure. If you want to change these, use the Navigation view, right-click on a page and click *Rename*. The page title will then be changed in all the navigation bars on your site.

Keep it simple

Many people, from beginners to professionals, make the mistake of putting too much material on a page. Remember that a computer screen is harder to read than a paper copy, so designs that might look fine on paper can be tiring on screen.

Some of the most effective Web sites use very simple designs with plain colours, a few well-chosen images and short, easy-to-read blocks of text. Some fonts are easier to read on screen than others (see page 13), so it's a good idea to use these for your text.

Keep your home page, in particular, uncluttered and easy to read. If you have large amounts of text or collections of images, it's best to place these on separate pages with links from the home page.

Keep it working

However spectacular a site looks, the most important thing is that it should actually work. Broken links, pictures that fail to download or that take much too long can completely spoil the effect of a site. It's really important to make sure your site runs smoothly and to keep checking that all the links work.

Web design help sites

You'll find links to useful sites discussing Web design at **www.usborne-quicklinks.com**

For example, there's a basic guide to Web design on the **Design Resource** Web site, produced for the WebExpress Web editor but with good advice for any Web designer

On the **WDVL** site there's a series of articles on designing attractive Web pages, quite technical in places but full of good sense.

And advice on the **Top Ten Mistakes in Web Design**: Jakob Nielsen is a leading Web design expert. Amazingly, this article was written in 1996 but is still very relevant today.

Cool Web sites and where to find them

You can continue to find good ideas for Web site designs by looking at other people's sites. Remember that good design isn't all about special effects, although they can make a site more attractive and impressive. The most effective sites are the ones which are elegant to look at and easy to use.

You can find links to all these sites at **www.usborne-quicklinks.com**

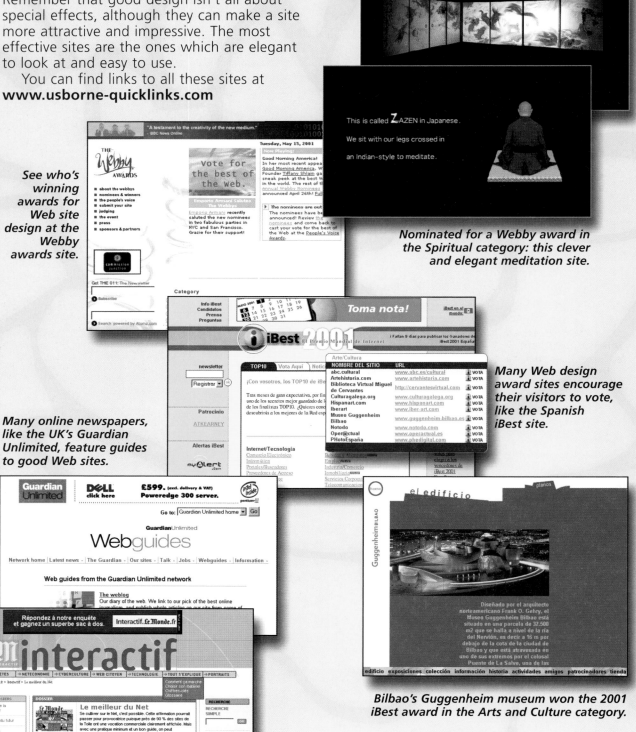

See who's winning awards for Web site design at the Webby awards site.

Nominated for a Webby award in the Spiritual category: this clever and elegant meditation site.

Many Web design award sites encourage their visitors to vote, like the Spanish iBest site.

Many online newspapers, like the UK's Guardian Unlimited, feature guides to good Web sites.

Bilbao's Guggenheim museum won the 2001 iBest award in the Arts and Culture category.

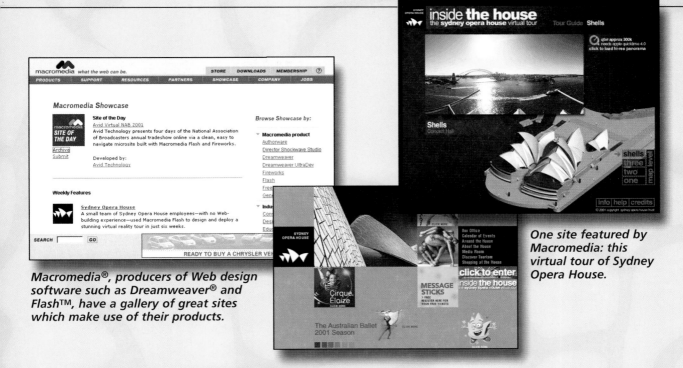

Macromedia®, producers of Web design software such as Dreamweaver® and Flash™, have a gallery of great sites which make use of their products.

One site featured by Macromedia: this virtual tour of Sydney Opera House.

Macromedia's international gallery features sites such as this Italian one for bonsai enthusiasts.

The Lynda.com Web site not only has some great Web design tips but also a specially selected gallery of inspiring sites.

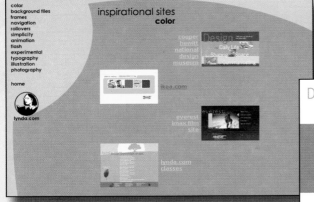

One of the sites featured on Lynda.com is New York's Cooper Hewitt Design Museum, using simple colours and images really effectively.

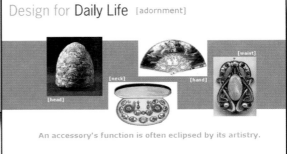

Glossary

Here is a list that explains some of the words you may come across while you are working on your Web site. Some of the words may have other meanings in other contexts; the meanings given in this list are specific to Web site design. Any word that appears in *italic* type is defined elsewhere in this glossary.

AIFF A *file format* used by Macintosh operating systems to create sound files.

alternative text Text description that appears when the mouse cursor is placed over a picture, *animation* or *hyperlink*.

anchor tag An *HTML* instruction which tells the *browser* to go to another Web page, and tells it where that page is located. It is used to create *hyperlinks*.

animation A moving image made by showing a series of pictures in quick succession.

applet A small program written in *Java*.

AU A sound *file format*. AU files can be played by all *browsers* but may sound crackly.

audio player A program that plays sound files.

bookmark A *hyperlink* within a Web page, for example to return to the top of the page.

broken link A *hyperlink* which no longer works because the linked Web page has been deleted or moved.

browser A program that enables your computer to find and view pages on the World Wide Web. It can also be used to check your own Web site as you are designing it.

clip art *Copyright*-free pictures that can be used for illustrating documents or Web pages.

compression Making a file smaller so that it takes less time to *download*.

copyright The legal rights of a person or organization over pictures, music or information they have created. You must obtain permission before reproducing copyright material.

digital Information recorded as a number code that can be processed by computers. It is also used to describe other devices which can process this code, such as digital cameras.

domain name The name part of a *URL*, for example Usborne in www.usborne.com

dots per inch The measure of *resolution* of a digital image.

download To copy Web pages, pictures or other files or programs from the Internet onto your computer.

encoder A program that converts sounds into the right *file format* to be used on a *Web site*.

encryption The process of converting information into a special code to keep it secret.

file format The way a program stores information, such as a picture or sound.

Flash™ A program that makes it possible to create animations and interactive features for Web pages.

frame One of a series of images that makes up an *animation*.

frames A way of dividing up a Web page into separate areas to manage large amounts of information. Now less widely used than *tables*.

FTP (File Transfer Protocol) Transerring files via the Internet to a *server,* so that anyone on the Internet can have access to them.

GIF (Graphics Interchange Format) A *compressed file format* used for pictures on Web pages.

GIF animation A way of creating an *animation* from a series of *GIF* files.

graphics program A program which allows you to create or manipulate images with a computer.

hit counter A device that counts how many times a *Web page* is visited.

home page The opening page of a *Web site,* or the main page from which you can go to other pages on the site.

host A computer, connected to the Internet, that stores files such as Web pages and makes them available to other Internet users.

hosting company A company that offers *Web space* to people or organizations who want to publish their Web site. See also **Web Presence Provider**.

hotspot An area of a picture which has been made into a *hyperlink*.

HTML (HyperText Mark-up Language) The language used to create Web pages. It contains coded instructions that tell a *browser* what to show on a Web page and how to show it.

hyperlink Also known as a link. A word, phrase or picture on a Web page that, when clicked, tells a *browser* to go to another part of a Web page, another page or another Web site.

icon A small picture which represents something else, such as a link to another part of your site.

ISP (Internet Service Provider) A company that sells or offers Internet connections, and may also provide *Web space*.

Java A programming language used to add animations, sounds and interactive features to Web pages.

JPEG (Joint Photographic Expert Group) A *compressed file format* used for photographs or complex images on Web pages.

keyword A word which describes the content of a Web site. Most *search engines* find sites by looking for keywords.

links page A page on a Web site with a list of links to other sites.

local link A *hyperlink* between pages on the same Web site.

MIDI (Musical Instrument Digital Interface) A sound *file format* used for recording sounds from an electronic musical instrument to a computer.

MP3 A highly *compressed* sound *file format* which still produces good quality sound.

pixel A tiny dot that is part of a picture. Everything that appears on a computer screen is made up of pixels.

public domain information Information that is not in *copyright* and is free for anyone to use.

remote link A *hyperlink* from one Web site to another.

resolution The number of *pixels* that make up a picture on a computer screen. High-resolution pictures look sharper than low-resolution ones.

scanner A device that converts pictures into *digital* images.

search engine A program that searches the Internet for Web pages containing particular words or phrases.

SSL (Secure Sockets Layer) A system which makes it possible to set up secure pages on a Web site. All information sent from the Web page to the site *server*, such as credit card details, will be *encrypted*.

server A powerful computer that carries out tasks for other computers on a network or on the Internet. Some servers are used to store and publish Web pages.

sound card A device that enables a computer to record sound and play it back.

table A way of arranging information or creating a structure for a Web page.

tag An *HTML* instruction that tells a *browser* how to display a certain part of a document.

thumbnail A small picture on a Web page which you can click on to see a larger version.

upload To copy files, such as Web pages, from your computer to another computer, generally a *server*, on the Internet.

URL (Uniform Resource Locator) The specific address of a Web site or page. Each Web site has its own unique URL.

WAV A sound *file format* developed by Microsoft®.

Web editor A program that helps you to create a Web page without having to know *HTML*.

Web Presence Provider A company that sells or offers *Web space*.

Web space Space provided by an *ISP* or other *Web Presence Provider* on their *server* for hosting a Web site.

WYSIWYG (What You See Is What You Get) Any software that allows you to create a document and see it on your computer screen exactly as it will appear when published.

Index

Acknowledgements

Every effort has been made to trace the copyright holders of the material in this book. If any rights have been omitted, the publishers offer their sincere apologies and will rectify this in any subsequent editions following notification.

Screen shots used with permission from Microsoft Corporation. Microsoft®, Microsoft® Windows®, Microsoft® Windows® 95, Microsoft® Windows®98, Microsoft® Windows® Me, Microsoft® Internet Explorer and Microsoft® FrontPage® are either registered trademarks or trademarks of Microsoft Corporation in the US and other countries.

p2-3   B Camara's: a collection of travel reports and photos by Benjamin Camara. Used with permission.
Citrus Cool Kids: Megan Berry ©2001. Used with permission.
Imperial War Museum: used with permission.
Planet Paige: design by Online Computer Distribution, www.kawartha.com Used with permission
Silver Midnight: created by Kristal Imatong Trevino Lee. Used with permission.
With thanks to AFP.

p4-5   Eviaggi.com, FC Barcelona and NHS Direct: used with permission.
Médecins sans Frontières: © used with permission.
Metropolitan Museum of Art: Mayan figure, The Michael C. Rockefeller Memorial Collection, Bequest of Nelson A. Rockefeller, 1979 (1979.206.1063). Photography by Schechter Lee © 1986 The Metropolitan Museum of Art, www.metmuseum.org © 2001 The Metropolitan Museum of Art.
Teenage Fanclub: design, Federal Bureau of Design (FBD); content, Columbia Records UK. Used with permission.
With thanks to Craig Williams and Gazeta.

p6-7   Modem used with thanks to 3Com, Inc.
Planet Paige, as before.
PC: Gateway Profile 3, used with permission.
With thanks to Macromedia®.

p8-9   Snapshots and flowers: Digital Vision.

p14-15   Clip art courtesy of Clip Art Warehouse.
Photos: Ian Britton, www.freefoto.com Used with permission.

p16-17   Photos: Ian Britton, as before.
Background: www.motzmotz.com/ backgrounds Used with permission.

p18-19   B Camara's, as before
Josep Fornell, Spanish rallye driver: used with permission.
Amy Miller Gray: ©2001 used with permission.
Web site of the Nieukerke family: used with permission.
Reinhardt family: Paul Reinhardt, used with permission.
Todounquillo, Gustavo Bazán: used with permission
Vrai Millenaire, Edwin Torres: used with permission.
With thanks to Bertacci and the Thiboutot family.

p20-21   Background and photos: www.motzmotz.com and Ian Britton as before.

p22-23   Hewlett Packard Photosmart C315 digital camera and Epson flatbed scanner, used with permission.
Icons: Clip Art Warehouse, as before.
Photos: Ian Britton, as before, except skier: Digital Vision.

p24-25   The Infamous Grouse Band is in no way associated with The Famous Grouse Brand. Band logo used on Web site with permission.

p30-31   Hewlett Packard Netserver LC 2000, used with permission.
Juno and the Juno logo are registered trademarks of Juno Online Services, Inc. Used with permission.
KataWeb: used with permission of KataWeb SpA.
Terra: Used with permission of Terra Networks SA.
Tiscali: used with permission of Tiscali SpA.
T-online and Wanadoo: used with permission.
Angelfire logo: ©2001 Angelfire, a Lycos Network site. All rights reserved.
Homestead: used with permission.
Yahoo! Geocities logo © 1994-2001 Yahoo! Inc. All rights reserved.
With thanks to Freeserve.

p32-33   Terrapin FTP: Terrapin Internet Ltd., used with permission.

p34-35   @U2: courtesy @U2/ Matt McGee.
FCBayern, the official Web site: used with permission.
Harry Potter: Warner Bros Online, used with permission.
Lara Croft Tomb Raider: Paramount Pictures, used with permission.
Leftfield Online: design, Kleber; content, Columbia Records UK. Used with permission.
Tinstar: used with permission.
With thanks to Björk, the Los Angeles Lakers, Olympique de Marseille and U2.

p36-37   CDex, with thanks to Albert L Faber.

p40-41   Java applet, from the Nieukerke family Web site, as before. Flash animation courtesy of Vasava Artworks SL.

p44-45   Comunn Gaidhlig Lunnainn: used with permission.

p48-49   Amazon.de GmbH, Apple Computer, Inc and Unicef: used with permission.
Médecins Sans Frontières: © used with permission.
With thanks to Société Céline SA, DaimlerChrysler, Paul Frank Industries and Renta4 SVB SA.

p50-51   With thanks to Amazon, Century21 and La Repubblica:

p52-53   Background and photos: www.motzmotz.com and Ian Britton as before.

p54-55   Comunn Gaidhlig Lunnainn: used with permission.
With thanks to Macromedia®.

p56-57   Imperial War Museum and Médecins Sans Frontières, as before.

p58-59   www.bonsaka.com, Guardian Unlimited Webguides, Le Monde interactif and Lynda.com: used with permission.
Guggenheim Museum: © FMGB Guggenheim Bilbao Museoa, Bilbao.
With thanks to the Cooper Hewitt Design Museum, Do-not-zzz, iBest awards, Macromedia®, Sydney Opera House and the Webby awards.

This edition produced for:
The Book People Ltd, Hall Wood Avenue, Haydock, St Helens WA11 9UL